LA CUCINA
ITALIANA

DELICIOUS

DESSERTS

LA CUCINA ITALIANA

DELICIOUS

DESSERTS

PRION

Published in the United Kingdom 1994 by
PRION,
an imprint of Multimedia Books Limited,
32-34 Gordon House Road, London NW5 1LP

Exclusive distribution in the USA by
Smithmark Publishers Inc.
16 East 32nd Street, New York, NY 10016

Managing Editor: Anne Johnson
Design: Megra Mitchell
Production: Hugh Allan

Copyright © Multimedia Books Limited 1994
Original recipes and pictures copyright © NEPI
La Cucina Italiana, **Via Mascheroni, 1-20123 Milan**

ISBN 0-8317-2157-X

10 9 8 7 6 5 4 3 2 1

Printed in Italy by New Interlitho

CONTENTS

PASTRIES

Italian pastries are a delight – both to the taste buds and to the eye. They can be simple or elaborate, dainty or gargantuan, old favorites or unusual new confections, suitable for a family meal or a special feast.
Rest assured, however, that whatever you choose,
it's guaranteed to be delicious.

Grape and Apple Cheesecake

Crostata di Mascarpone all'Uva e Mela

To serve 8

1 cup all-purpose flour

¹/₄ cup sugar

a pinch of salt

¹/₂ cup butter

4 egg yolks

grated peel of 1 lemon

a little butter and flour for tart pan

7 ounces mascarpone cheese

¹/₂ cup powdered sugar

2 tablespoons brandy

20 small Amaretti macaroons

a large bunch green grapes

1 apple

5 tablespoons sugar

5 mint leaves

Preparation and cooking time: about 1¹/₂ hours

To make the dough, put the sifted flour, sugar and salt together in a bowl. Add the butter, cut into small cubes. Rub it in with your fingers until the mixture resembles coarse bread crumbs. Add 2 egg yolks and the lemon peel. Roll the dough into a ball, wrap it in plastic wrap and leave it in the refrigerator for 30 minutes.

Meanwhile, preheat the oven to 375°F. Grease and flour a 10-inch tart pan with a smooth bottom and fluted sides.

Roll out the dough and line the pan, pricking the bottom with a fork. Bake in the oven for about 20 minutes or until crisp and golden. Leave to cool in the pan.

Now prepare the filling. Beat the cheese and sifted powdered sugar together, incorporating the 2 egg yolks, one at a time. Stir in the brandy.

Crumble the macaroons finely. When the pie shell is cool, take it out of the tart pan and set it on a plate. Sprinkle the macaroons over the bottom, then pour in the filling. Wash

and dry the grapes and arrange them on top together with some thin slices of apple.

Dissolve the remaining sugar in 1 tablespoon of water over low heat. When it is a thick syrup, brush it, still hot, over the fruit. Decorate the center of the cake with the mint leaves and keep it in a cool place until required. Serve within a couple of hours.

Plum Turnovers

Mezzelune alla Marmellata

To serve 6-8

3 cups all-purpose flour, plus a little extra for the work surface and baking sheet

¹/₄ teaspoon baking powder

¹/₂ cup sugar

grated peel of ¹/₂ lemon

2 eggs

1 tablespoon vanilla sugar

6 tablespoons butter, plus a little extra for greasing the baking sheet

2 tablespoons anise-flavored liqueur

³/₄-1 cup plum jam

powdered sugar

Preparation and cooking time: about 1¹/₂ hours

Sift the flour and baking powder together. Add the sugar, and the grated lemon peel. Stir and then make a well in the center. Place the eggs, vanilla sugar, butter (cut into little pieces) and the anise-flavored liqueur in the well. Combine with the flour to form a firm, smooth dough. Preheat the oven to 350°F.

Dust the work surface with a little flour and roll out the dough to a thickness of ¹/₄ inch. Cut into 3-inch circles with a fluted cookie cutter. Place 1 teaspoon of plum jam on each piece of dough and fold each circle in half, pressing the edges to seal.

Place the crescents on a buttered baking sheet which has been sprinkled with a little flour. Make sure they are not too close together as they will

spread during baking.

Bake in the oven for 20 minutes. Leave to cool and sprinkle with a little powdered sugar. Arrange on a dish and serve.

Strawberry and Apple Pie

Pie di Fragole e Mele

To serve 6

12 ounces apples

3 tablespoons butter

¹/₄ cup sugar

3 tablespoons maraschino liqueur

12 ounces strawberries

2 soft Amaretti macaroons

6 soft ladyfingers

7 ounces frozen puff pastry dough, thawed

1 egg, beaten, for glazing

Preparation and cooking time: about 1 hour

Peel and core the apples, then cut them into small segments. In a large saucepan, melt the butter. Add the apples, sprinkle with sugar and brown over high heat. Cook for about 2 minutes, then moisten with the maraschino liqueur. Evaporate the liquid completely, and leave to cool.

Meanwhile, preheat the oven to 400°F. Hull the strawberries, rinse and dry well. Cut into small segments and place in a round pie dish, together with the cold apples and the crumbled Amaretti cookies and ladyfingers.

Roll out the dough and use it to cover the pie dish, making sure it adheres well to the edges. Cut off the excess dough and use the trimmings to make decorations on top of the pie. Arrange these on the dough, glaze with the beaten egg and bake in the hot oven for about 30 minutes.

Place the pie dish on a serving plate and serve the pie straight from the dish.

Grape and Apple Cheesecake

Prune and Apple Tart

Crostata di Prugne e Mele

To serve 10

½ pound prunes, pitted

½ cup rum

¾ cup plus 2 tablespoons butter, plus extra for greasing the pan

2½ cups all-purpose flour, plus extra for the work surface

1 egg

9 tablespoons sugar

½ teaspoon vanilla extract

a pinch of salt

1¾ pounds apples

2 tablespoons butter

juice of ½ lemon

about 20 slivered almonds

1 egg, beaten

powdered sugar

Preparation and cooking time:
about 2 hours

Soak the prunes in the rum for about 1 hour.

Work the butter and flour together, then place on a work surface and make a well in the center. Break the egg into the well and add 6 tablespoons of the sugar, vanilla and salt. Mix quickly, using your fingertips so the butter doesn't become too soft, which would make the dough lose its body. Roll the dough into a ball, wrap in plastic wrap and refrigerate for 30 minutes.

Preheat the oven to 375°F. To make the filling, peel and core the apples and dice finely. Place in a saucepan with the butter, lemon juice, remaining 3 tablespoons sugar and a little cold water. Cover the pan and cook the apples over high heat for 7 minutes, then add the prunes and the rum they were soaked in. Cook until the prunes are quite dry and the apples are pulpy, then leave to cool.

On a lightly floured work surface, roll out the dough into a circle ¼ inch thick. Use it to line a greased 10-inch

tart pan, cutting off the excess dough. Pour the cooked fruit into the tart pan.

Reroll the dough trimmings, then, using a fluted cutter, cut into ½-inch wide strips. Arrange these in a lattice pattern on the fruit and fill the spaces with slivered almonds. Brush the dough with beaten egg and sift over a light dusting of powdered sugar. Bake in the hot oven for about 40 minutes. Serve the tart at room temperature.

Peach and Macaroon Pie

Crostata di Pesche all'Amaretto

To serve 6-8

a little butter and flour for pie dish

1 cup all-purpose flour

a pinch of salt

¼ cup sugar

grated peel of ½ lemon

1 egg yolk

¼ cup butter, softened

1 tablespoon dry vermouth

12 small Amaretti macaroons

6 tablespoons peach jam

1 tablespoon apricot brandy

2 large yellow peaches

1 tablespoon Amaretto liqueur

a few sprigs of red currants

Preparation and cooking time:
about 1 hour, plus cooling

Preheat the oven to 375°F. Butter and flour a round 10-inch pie dish.

Sift the flour and add the salt, sugar and the grated lemon peel. Make a well in the center and add the egg yolk, the softened butter, cut into small pieces, and the vermouth. Knead rapidly into a smooth dough, then roll out and line the prepared dish with it; prick the bottom of the dough with a fork. Crumble 7 macaroons over. Set aside 2 tablespoons of jam, place the rest in a bowl and stir in the apricot brandy. Spread evenly over the crumbs.

Peel, halve and pit the peaches, then cut them into equal slices and arrange them in a circle, slightly overlapping on the dough. In the center, put the remaining macaroons and sprinkle them with the Amaretto liqueur. Bake for about 40 minutes.

Remove the pie from the oven and let it cool in the dish, then place it on a large round plate. Melt the remaining jam over low heat, strain it through a fine strainer and brush the peach slices and the macaroons with it. As soon as the glaze has cooled and is firm, garnish the pie with sprigs of red currants and serve.

May Evening Tart

Crostata "Sera di Maggio"

To serve 8

¹/₄ cup all-purpose flour, plus extra for the dish

³/₄ cup sugar

grated peel of ¹/₂ lemon

a pinch of salt

6 tablespoons butter, softened, plus extra for the dish

1 small egg

1 tablespoon unflavored gelatin

1¹/₄ pounds ripe strawberries

¹/₂ cup orange liqueur

²/₃ cup whipping cream

a few mint leaves for garnish

Preparation and cooking time:
about 1 hour, plus 3-4 hours chilling

Mix the flour, ¹/₄ cup of the sugar, the grated lemon peel and salt together and make a well in the center. Cut the softened butter into small pieces and place in the well with the egg; mix quickly to form a smooth dough. Roll it into a ball, wrap it in waxed paper or plastic wrap and let it rest in the refrigerator for about 30 minutes.

Meanwhile, preheat the oven to 350°F. Butter and flour a round quiche dish 9 inches in diameter. Roll out enough pastry to line the dish and prick it with a fork; cover it with a sheet of foil and place a few dried beans on top. Bake the dough for about 30 minutes. Remove the beans and foil and let the pie shell cool inside the dish.

Dissolve the gelatin in a little cold water. Remove the stems from 1 pound of the strawberries, rinse them in very cold water, drain well, then cut them into small pieces. Place them in a

blender or food processor together with the remaining sugar and purée them, first at low speed, then at high speed for a couple of minutes.

Heat the orange liqueur in a saucepan; remove it from the heat and, while still hot, fold in the gelatin, stirring until it is completely dissolved. Add the strawberries and stir the mixture for 30 seconds longer.

Turn out the tart shell onto a serving dish and pour the strawberry mixture over, distributing it evenly. Keep the tart in the refrigerator for 3-4 hours or, even better, overnight, to set the filling.

A short time before serving, beat the whipping cream until stiff, then put it in a pastry bag and decorate, finishing off with the remaining strawberries, rinsed but not chopped, and a few mint leaves. Serve immediately.

Prune and Apple Tart (far left) and
Peach and Macaroon Pie (below)

Pear Tart

Flan di Pere

To serve 6

¹/₂ cup all-purpose flour

6 tablespoons butter, softened

3 tablespoons sugar

¹/₃ cup finely chopped hazelnuts

¹/₂ teaspoon vanilla extract

a pinch of salt

3 large red pears

1 cup dry red wine

1¹/₂ cups sugar

1 cinnamon stick

a few black peppercorns

1 tablespoon unflavored gelatin, soaked in cold water

Preparation and cooking time:
about 1 hour 20 minutes

Quickly knead the flour with the softened butter, sugar, chopped hazelnuts, vanilla and salt dissolved in 4 tablespoons water. Leave the dough to rest in a cool place for 30 minutes.

Meanwhile, peel and halve the pears. Bring the wine to a boil with 1 cup water, the sugar, cinnamon and peppercorns. Add the pears and cook for 6 minutes. Drain and leave to cool while you reduce the poaching syrup by half. Stir in the gelatin, making sure it has dissolved completely, then leave to cool.

Preheat the oven to 425°. Roll out the dough to a thickness of ¹/₈ inch, prick with a fork, then use it to line the bottom and sides of a fluted 9-inch tart pan. Cover with aluminum foil, fill the pan with baking beans to prevent the dough from puffing up during baking, and bake in the hot oven for about 20 minutes. Leave to cool, then fan out the pears on the cool tart shell, pour the wine glaze over and serve.

Mascarpone Gougère (top) and
Pear Tart (bottom)

Mascarpone Gougère

Gougère al Mascarpone

To serve 6

¼ cup butter, plus a little for greasing

a pinch of salt

1 cup all-purpose flour

3 eggs

1 cup chopped mixed candied fruits

sugar crystals

6 tablespoons sugar

2 egg yolks, beaten

⅔ cup mascarpone cheese

port wine

5 ounces semisweet chocolate, chopped or grated into flakes

Preparation and cooking time:
about 1 hour 20 minutes

Preheat the oven to 400°F. Bring to a boil ⅔ cup water with ¼ cup butter and the salt. Tip in the flour all at once and keep the pan on the heat, stirring continuously, until the mixture dries out slightly. Transfer to the bowl of an electric mixer fitted with a dough hook and leave to cool. Beat in the eggs, one at a time, then the candied fruit.

On a greased baking sheet, place spoonfuls of the choux paste, touching each other to form an 8-inch crown. Sprinkle with sugar crystals, then bake in the hot oven for 10 minutes. Reduce the heat to 350°F and bake for 20 minutes longer.

To make the filling, cook the sugar with a drop of water to a temperature of 235°F on a candy thermometer. Gradually pour the syrup onto the egg yolks in a heatproof bowl, then add the mascarpone cheese and a small glass of port wine. Place the filling in the center of the gougère crown and decorate with chopped or flaked chocolate.

Raspberry Tart

Crostata ai Lamponi

To serve 6

2¾ cups all-purpose flour

10 tablespoons butter, softened

¼ cup sugar

a pinch of salt

2 eggs

½ teaspoon vanilla extract

2 tablespoons all-purpose flour

1 tablespoon cornstarch

orange liqueur

4 ounces semisweet chocolate

4 ounces raspberries

powdered sugar

Preparation and cooking time:
about 1 hour

To make the tart shell, put the flour, softened butter, 2 ounces of the sugar, salt and 6 tablespoons cold water in a bowl and quickly work together to form a dough. Wrap in plastic wrap and refrigerate for 30 minutes.

Meanwhile, make the filling. With an electric mixer, beat the eggs with the remaining sugar and vanilla until light and creamy, then sift in the flour and cornstarch, a little at a time, and add a dash of liqueur. Break the chocolate into a bowl and melt it in a warm bain-marie.

Preheat the oven to 350°F. Roll out the dough very thinly and use it to line a 10-inch tart pan, crimping up the border. Line with aluminum foil and fill with dried baking beans to prevent the dough from puffing up during baking. Bake in the preheated oven for 15 minutes, then take the tart shell out of the oven and remove the paper and beans. Increase the oven temperature to 425°F. Leaving the tart shell in the tin, fill it with melted chocolate, half the raspberries and the filling. Decorate with the remaining raspberries, dust liberally with sifted powdered sugar and return to the hot oven for about 10 minutes, checking that the sugar does not burn.

Unmold the tart onto a serving plate and serve cold, dusted with powdered sugar.

Raspberry Tart

Amaretto Tart

Crostata all'Amaretto

To serve 8

2¹/₂ cups all-purpose flour

¹/₂ cup butter, softened and diced

1 egg, plus 6 extra yolks

1 cup powdered sugar

¹/₂ teaspoon vanilla extract

12 soft Amaretti macaroons

1¹/₄ cups mascarpone cheese

flour and butter for the work surface and pan

13 small Amaretti macaroons

rum

1¹/₄ cups whipping cream

cocoa powder

Preparation and cooking time:
about 1 hour 40 minutes

First make the dough. Mix the flour with the butter together and make a

well in the center. Add the egg and one yolk, then add the powdered sugar and vanilla. Knead quickly so that the butter does not become too warm, then form the mixture into a dough, wrap in plastic wrap and refrigerate for about 30 minutes.

Now prepare the filling. Crush the 12 soft Amaretti macaroons in a food processor, pulsing the motor for only 1 or 2 seconds so they are not crushed too finely. In a bowl, combine the mascarpone, 5 egg yolks and crushed macaroons. Mix together until smooth and blended.

Preheat the oven to 400°F. Take the dough out of the refrigerator, remove the plastic wrap and lightly flour the work surface. Roll out the dough into a circle ¹/₈ inch thick. Grease and flour a 10-inch tart pan and line it with the dough. Fill with the cheese mixture and bake in the preheated oven for about 50 minutes. Remove the tart from the oven, unmold it onto a wire rack and leave to cool.

Just before serving, decorate the tart with small Amaretti macaroons sprinkled with rum. Whip the cream and, using a pastry bag with a fluted tip, pipe on rosettes of cream. Sift over a dusting of cocoa and serve.

Raisin and Pine Nut Tart

Crostata di Uvetta e Pinoli

To serve 8

12 ounces frozen piecrust dough

flour and butter for the work surface and pan

²/₃ cup raisins

¹/₂ glass rum

¹/₃ cup pine nuts

6 egg yolks

³/₄ cup sugar

³/₄ cup whipping cream

¹/₂ teaspoon vanilla extract

powdered sugar for dusting

Preparation and cooking time:
about 50 minutes, plus thawing the dough

Thaw the dough and soak the raisins the rum.

When the dough has thawed,

preheat the oven to 375°F. On a floured surface, roll out the dough. Grease and flour a 10½-inch tart pan and line it with the dough, pinching it up along the border.

Drain the raisins from the rum, squeeze dry and lay over the dough. Place the pine nuts on top.

In a bowl, beat the egg yolks with the sugar, cream and vanilla. Pour this mixture over the raisins and pine nuts and bake the tart in the preheated oven for about 45 minutes. Unmold and serve warm or cold, with a dusting of powdered sugar.

Pear Cake

Torta di Pere

To serve 8

14 tablespoons butter, softened

1¼ cups powdered sugar, plus a little extra for dusting

3 eggs

1 cup all-purpose flour

½ cup cornstarch

½ teaspoon vanilla extract

rum extract

grated peel of 1 lemon

1 lb 2 oz pears

butter and flour for the pan

Preparation and cooking time: about 1¼ hours

Preheat the oven to 375°F. With an electric mixer, beat the softened butter with the powdered sugar until soft and fluffy. Add the eggs and, when they are completely amalgamated, sift in the flour and cornstarch. Flavor with the vanilla, 3-4 drops of rum extract and the grated peel of a well-washed lemon.

For a perfect tart, choose absolutely ripe pears. If they are underripe, they will not bake properly, and if overripe, they will give off too much juice during baking.

Peel the pears and slice thinly. Grease and flour a 10-inch springform cake pan. Add about half the pears to the egg mixture, pour into the pan and arrange the remaining pears on the surface. Bake in the preheated oven for

about 70 minutes.

Unmold the cake onto a serving dish and leave to cool slightly. Sift a thin layer of powdered sugar over and serve. The cake should be eaten almost as soon as it comes out of the oven.

Amaretto Tart (opposite), *Raisin and Pine Nut Tart* (top) and *Pear Cake* (above)

Fruit Vol-au-Vent

Sfogliata alla Frutta

To serve 8

1 lb 2 ounces frozen puff pastry dough

1 cup plus 2 tablespoons milk

grated peel of 1 lemon

2 egg yolks

6 tablespoons sugar

$^{1}/_{2}$ teaspoon vanilla extract

2 tablespoons all-purpose flour

flour and butter for the work surface and baking sheet

1 egg, beaten, for glazing

1 pound plums

14 ounces apricots

10 ounces peaches

3 ounces strawberries

1 slice of watermelon, about 1 pound

$^{1}/_{2}$ cup whipping cream

Preparation and cooking time: about 2 hours

Make the custard sauce while you thaw the dough. Heat the milk with the lemon peel. In a bowl, mix the egg yolks with the sugar, vanilla and flour. Gradually stir in the hot, but not boiling, milk, then return the custard to the saucepan you used for the milk and, stirring continuously to avoid lumps, simmer the custard sauce over very low heat for 3 to 4 minutes. Then take the pan off the heat and leave to cool.

Preheat the oven to 400°F. On a lightly floured surface, roll out the dough to a thickness of about $^{1}/_{4}$ inch, then cut out two 10-inch circles. Cut out a $1^{1}/_{4}$-inch border from one circle. Brush the larger circle with beaten egg and lay the border on top to make a vol-au-vent. Brush again with egg, then transfer to a greased baking sheet and bake in the preheated oven for about 25 minutes.

Meanwhile, pit and hull all the fruit. Reserve almost half the plums and one-third of the apricots, and cut the rest into small pieces. Scoop out the watermelon seeds.

Whip the cream until very stiff and mix it into the cold custard sauce. To assemble the vol-au-vent, place the cool pastry shell on a serving plate, then fill it with pieces of fruit, almost all the watermelon and the custard sauce. Decorate with the remaining fruit. Keep it in the refrigerator until ready to serve

Cherry Puff

Sfogliata di Vignola

To serve 6

14 ounces frozen puff pastry dough

$1^{1}/_{4}$ cups milk

$^{1}/_{2}$ teaspoon vanilla extract

grated peel of 1 lemon

3 egg yolks

7 tablespoons sugar

2 tablespoons all-purpose flour

11 ounces cherries

butter for greasing

1 tablespoon powdered sugar

Preparation and cooking time: about 55 minutes, plus thawing the dough

Thaw the dough. Meanwhile, prepare the pastry cream. Heat the milk with the vanilla and lemon peel. In a bowl,

beat the egg yolks with the sugar and flour. Gradually pour in the hot, but not boiling, milk, stirring to prevent lumps from forming. Return the mixture to the milk pan and set over very low heat. Simmer for 3 to 4 minutes, stirring continuously, then take off the heat and leave to cool.

Preheat the oven to 400°F. Rinse the cherries, drain well and pit with a cherry pitter. Roll out the dough into 2 equal rectangles. Spread the cold pastry cream over one and scatter the cherries over. Cover with the other dough rectangle and seal the edges so the filling does not seep out.

Place the cherry puff on a greased baking sheet and bake in the preheated oven for about 45 minutes. Remove from the oven as soon as it is puffed up and baked through and transfer to a serving plate. Serve slightly warm, sprinkled with powdered sugar.

Chocolate Tartlets

Tartelette Farcite

To make 20

---

¹/₂ cup butter

1³/₄ cups flour, plus extra for work surface

1¹/₂ cups powdered sugar

---

almond extract

---

1 cup mascarpone cheese

---

2 tablespoons kirsch

---

grated peel of 1 orange

---

5 ounces semisweet chocolate

Preparation and cooking time: about 1 hour

First prepare the tartlet shells (This can be done the day before.) Mix the butter with the flour and sugar, then place on the work surface and make a well in the center. Pour 3 tablespoons cold water and a few drops of almond extract into the center and knead quickly, using only your fingertips, so the butter doesn't become too warm. Wrap the dough in plastic wrap and refrigerate for about 30 minutes. Preheat the oven to 400°F.

Roll out the dough on a lightly floured work surface into an ¹/₈-inch thick circle, then use it to line twenty 2 ¹/₂-inch tartlet pans. Arrange these on a baking sheet and bake in the hot oven for about 10 minutes. Remove the tartlet shells from the oven, unmold them and leave to cool.

Meanwhile, prepare the filling. Put the mascarpone cheese in a bowl and sift in the remaining powdered sugar from a height. Mix together and flavor with the kirsch, orange peel and 1 ¹/₂ ounces of the chocolate, grated. Put the filling in a pastry bag fitted with a plain tip and pipe it into the tartlet shells.

Melt the remaining chocolate in a bain-marie and leave to cool almost completely, without hardening again. Place in a parchment decorating cone and decorate the tartlets. As each one is ready, place it on a serving plate and serve immediately.

Fruit Vol-au-vent (opposite), Cherry Puff (top) and Chocolate Tartlets (right)

FRUIT

Fruit must have been Man's earliest dessert. It is certainly one of the most versatile ingredients we have on offer and can be used in a multitude of ways. Modern transportation makes fresh fruit easily obtainable all year round, regardless of the season. With all the options available, the only problem is what to do with it. The choice is yours ...

DESSERTS

Netted Plums

Prugne nella Rete

To serve 4

butter and flour for the work surface and pan

2 tablespoons butter

3 eggs, plus 1 extra yolk

2 cups sugar

grated peel of 1 lemon

a little vanilla sugar

¹/₂ cup cornstarch

1 cup all-purpose flour

10 large yellow plums

¹/₂ cup dry white wine

²/₃ cup plum jam

³/₄ cup Amaretto liqueur

Preparation and cooking time: about 2 hours

Preheat the oven to 350°F. To make the cake base, grease and flour a 9-inch dome-shaped cake pan. Melt the butter and leave it to cool while beating together the 3 whole eggs and the yolk with 1 cup of the sugar, until the mixture is light and fluffy. Stir in the grated lemon peel, vanilla sugar, cornstarch and most of the sifted flour. Lastly, add the cool melted butter.

Pour the batter into the prepared cake pan and bake it in the oven for 35 minutes, or until a skewer inserted into the center comes out clean. Cool on a wire rack.

While the cake is baking, wash and dry the plums, then cut them in half, remove the pits and place them in a pan in a single layer. Sprinkle with 2 tablespoons of sugar, add the white wine and cook them over medium heat with the lid on for 5 minutes. Take them out of the pan and drain them on paper towels. Add the plum jam and half the liqueur to the juice left in the pan. Stir over low heat until it becomes a thick syrup.

When the cake is cool, cut it into 3 layers, moisten them with the remaining liqueur, then spread with the jam mixture (reserving 2 tablespoons) and reassemble the cake on a serving plate. Spread the remaining jam on top and cover it with the cooked plum halves. Leave it in a cool place (not the refrigerator) while you prepare the caramel.

To make the caramel, place the remaining sugar and 3 tablespoons of water over low heat, stirring gently at first until the sugar is completely dissolved. Cook until the sugar caramelizes. Dip a wooden spoon into the caramel and run it crisscross fashion over all the plums, like an irregular net. Serve immediately.

Oranges in Orange Liqueur

Arance al Orange Liqueur

To serve 4

6 large ripe oranges, washed

6 sugar cubes

4 tablespoons orange liqueur

Preparation and cooking time: about 30 minutes, plus 30 minutes chilling

Pierce the washed oranges all over with a needle. Rub every side of a sugar cube over each orange. Place the sugar in a saucepan. Peel the oranges, remove all the pith and divide them into segments in a bowl. Squeeze any juice remaining in the peel over the sugar cubes.

Heat the sugar cubes gently until they dissolve. When a light syrup has formed, remove the pan from the heat and pour in the orange liqueur. Stir and leave to cool. Pour the liquid over the orange segments and refrigerate for 30 minutes before serving.

If you like, you can place the oranges in individual bowls and garnish to taste.

Bananas with Pistachios

Banane "Rosate" al Pistacchio

To serve 4

4 ripe bananas

2 tablespoons sugar

4 tablespoons rum

2 tablespoons shelled pistachio nuts

a pinch of salt

5 tablespoons red fruit or rose hip jam

4-5 rose petals

Preparation time: about 20 minutes

Peel the bananas and halve them lengthwise. Arrange them on a large dish and sprinkle the sugar and rum over. Leave to stand in a cool place.

Meanwhile, parboil the pistachios in salted water for a couple of minutes. Peel them while they are still hot and chop them finely. Put the jam into a bowl and stir until it is smooth. Place it in the center of a serving dish and arrange the bananas around it. Pour the rum marinade over the bananas and top with the pistachios.

Garnish with 4-5 fresh rose petals (if available) and serve immediately.

Netted Plums

Strawberry Mold

Sformato di Fragole

To serve 6

13 ounces strawberries

³/₄ cup sugar

juice of ¹/₂ lemon

1 cup milk

lemon peel

2 egg yolks

¹/₄ cup all-purpose flour

¹/₂ teaspoon vanilla extract

²/₃ cup heavy cream

soft ladyfingers

4 egg whites

a pinch of salt

¹/₃ cup superfine sugar

Preparation and cooking time:
about 1 hour, plus chilling

Hull and wash 10 ounces of the strawberries, reserving the rest for decoration. Place in a bowl and sprinkle ¹/₄ cup of the sugar and the lemon juice. Cover and leave to marinate in a cool place.

To make the pastry cream, heat the milk with a strip of well-washed lemon peel. In a bowl, mix the egg yolks with sugar, the flour and vanilla. Pour in the hot, but not boiling, milk in a steady stream, pour the mixture back into the milk pan and set over low heat. Simmer, stirring continuously, for

3 to 4 minutes. Take off the heat and leave to cool, stirring from time to time to prevent a skin from forming.

To assemble the dessert, whip the cream very stiffly and fold it into the pastry cream. Remove the strawberries from the marinade and brush the ladyfingers with the liquid.

In a bowl, make alternating layers of ladyfingers, marinated strawberries and pastry cream, ending with a layer of ladyfingers. Cover with plastic wrap and chill in the refrigerator for at least 6 hours.

Shortly before serving, make the meringue. Preheat the oven to 475°F. Beat the egg whites with the salt until very firm, then delicately fold in the superfine sugar. Place this mixture in a pastry bag fitted with a fluted tip. Invert the dessert onto an ovenproof serving dish and pipe the meringue all over it. Place it in the oven until just lightly browned, decorate with the remaining strawberries and serve immediately.

Melon Bavarian Cream

Bavarese di Melone

To serve 8-10

1¹/₂ tablespoons unflavored gelatin

1 perfectly ripe, medium melon

6 tablespoons sugar

2 ounces red currants

2 tablespoons vanilla sugar

1 cup whipping cream

4 tablespoons strawberry jam

Preparation and cooking time:
about 1¹/₄ hours, plus at least 2 hours chilling

Dissolve the gelatin in cold water. Wash and dry the melon, then halve it and remove the seeds. Remove the pulp with a spoon, without piercing the skin which will be used as a container.

Place the pulp in a saucepan and add the sugar and the red currants. Place the saucepan over the heat and, stirring occasionally with a wooden spoon, simmer gently until the mixture has the consistency of jam, making sure it does not stick to the bottom of the pan.

Remove from the heat, stir the mixture for a couple of minutes and pour it into a bowl. While it is still warm, stir in the vanilla sugar and the gelatin. Mix well to dissolve the gelatin, then let the mixture cool. Whip the cream and fold it into the melon cream when it is cool but not yet firm, mixing with a motion from top to bottom, rather than round and round (to prevent the cream from going flat). Pour the strawberry jam into a small bowl and stir vigorously with a spoon to make it smooth.

Spread a layer of the melon Bavarian cream in each halved melon shell and pour some of the strawberry jam over each layer. Refrigerate for at least 2 hours or until set, then cut each half into 4 or 5 slices, using a very sharp knife. Arrange the slices on a serving plate and serve.

Fruit and Nut Surprise

Pesche ai Pinoli

To serve 4

---

4 ripe, equal-sized peaches

---

a knob of butter

---

1 clove

2-inch piece lemon peel

---

2 tablespoons sugar

---

6 tablespoons brandy

---

8 tablespoons pine nuts

Preparation and cooking time:
about 45 minutes

Remove the stems from the peaches, then wash and dry them. Cut them in half with a small, sharp knife and remove the pits.

Melt a large knob of butter in a saucepan, then arrange the 8 peach halves on the bottom of the pan, cut sides down. Fry very gently for a few moments with the pan uncovered, then add the clove and the piece of lemon peel. Sprinkle the fruit with the sugar and moisten with the brandy. Move the pan slightly to make sure the peaches do not stick to the bottom, then lower the heat to the minimum, cover and cook the peaches for about 20 minutes until they are poached and glazed.

Place the peaches, cut sides upward, on a serving dish and, in the hollow of each, place a spoonful of pine nuts. Reduce the cooking liquid slightly, then strain it directly onto the fruit.

Serve immediately while still hot – although peaches prepared in this way are also excellent lukewarm.

Strawberry Mold (far left); **Melon Bavarian Cream** *(above)*

Semolina and Pear Molds

Sformatini Semolino e Pere

To serve 6

2¹/₂ cups milk

1 cup sugar, plus a few extra spoonfuls for the molds

¹/₂ teaspoon vanilla extract

grated peel of ¹/₂ lemon

1 cup plus 2 tablespoons semolina

1¹/₄ pounds pears

¹/₄ cup butter

1 tablespoon rum

4 egg yolks

4 ounces fresh or frozen raspberries

¹/₂ cup whipping cream

Preparation and cooking time:
about 45 minutes

Bring the milk to a boil, then add 6 tablespoons of the sugar, the vanilla and the lemon peel. Scatter in all the semolina from above, mixing well to avoid lumps from forming. Cook for 10 minutes, stirring continuously, stirring in one direction.

Peel and core the pears and dice the flesh finely. Heat 2 tablespoons of the butter with 1 tablespoon of the remaining sugar in a skillet. Add the diced pears and sauté for about 3 minutes, taking care that they do not disintegrate. Flavor with the rum, then take off the heat.

Grease 6 crème caramel molds or ramekins and coat with a sprinkling of sugar. Add the egg yolks to the semolina mixture, one by one, stirring until completely blended in. Pour 2 tablespoons of semolina into each mold, then make a layer of half the pears. Repeat the layering, ending with a layer of semolina.

Stand the molds in a bain-marie of hot, but not boiling, water, and cook in the oven at 375°F for 30 minutes.

Meanwhile, prepare the sauce. Purée the raspberries in a blender with the remaining sugar and the cream. Pour into a small saucepan and heat the sauce until thickened.

Carefully turn out the semolina molds, taking care not to break them, then pour over the hot sauce. Serve at once.

Baked Peaches

Pesche al Forno

To serve 8

4 large peaches, about 1³/₄ pounds

3 tablespoons sugar

1 glass full-bodied red wine

2 tablespoons blanched almonds

¹/₃ cup shelled hazelnuts

8 Amaretti cookies

1 cup whipping cream

vanilla ice cream

Preparation and cooking time:
about 1 hour

Preheat the oven to 400°F. Halve the peaches along the lines running down their sides and remove the pits. Arrange the unpeeled peach halves, rounded sides up, in a baking dish. Sprinkle with the sugar and moisten with the wine. Bake in the preheated oven for about 20 minutes.

Meanwhile, finely crush the almonds, hazelnuts and Amaretti macaroons in a food processor, then tip them onto a sheet of wax paper. Take the peaches out of the oven, drain off the cooking liquid, then arrange the peaches on a serving plate and leave to cool.

Whip the cream until very stiff. Place the ice cream in a bowl and leave to soften slightly. With an ice-cream scoop, make 8 balls, then roll them in the crushed nut mixture. Place a ball in the cavity of each peach half.

Put the whipped cream into a pastry bag with a fluted tip, and pipe a ribbon of cream around the balls of ice cream. Serve immediately.

Semolina and Pear Molds (left) and
Baked Peaches (below)

Tropical Fig Delight

Fichi Speziati con Ribes e Gelato

To serve 6

2¼ pounds fresh figs, not overripe

½ cup sugar

⅓ cup golden raisins

a large pinch of ground cinnamon

a large pinch of ground ginger

a few whole cloves

6 tablespoons brandy

pared peel of 1 lemon

12 thin slices fruit cake or loaf

red currants

6 scoops vanilla ice cream

Preparation and cooking time: about 40 minutes, plus 1 hour marinating

Using a small, sharp knife, peel the figs. Cut each one into 4 or 6 pieces according to size and place in a stainless steel saucepan. Add the sugar, golden raisins, cinnamon, ginger and a few cloves. Pour 2 tablespoons of the brandy over. Cut a 3-inch piece of lemon peel into needle-fine strips and add to the saucepan. Cover the mixture and leave it in a cool place for about 1 hour or so.

Cook the figs over low heat for about 15 minutes from the moment the liquid begins to simmer. Keep the pan uncovered and stir gently from time to time. Immerse the saucepan in cold water to cool quickly.

Arrange the fruit cake in a glass bowl and pour the remaining brandy over. Spread the fig mixture on top and cover. Keep in the refrigerator until it is time to serve, then sprinkle some stemmed and rinsed red currants on top and add scoops of vanilla ice cream.

Strawberry Tart

Torta Ripiena alle Fragole

To serve 12

4 eggs, plus 2 extra yolks

1¹/₂ cups sugar

a pinch of salt

1¹/₂ teaspoons vanilla extract

1¹/₄ cups all-purpose flour

butter and flour for the pan

1¹/₄ cups milk

grated peel of 1 lemon

9 ounces strawberries, plus 6 extra for decoration

6 tablespoons maraschino liqueur

1¹/₄ cups whipping cream

powdered sugar

Preparation and cooking time: about 2 hours

First make a cake for the bottom layer. (This can be done 3 or 4 days in advance.) Preheat the oven to 350°F. Beat the 4 eggs with half the sugar, the salt, and ¹/₂ teaspoon of the vanilla, using an electric mixer, until a ribbon consistency forms. Sift in the flour from a height, then fold it in.

Grease a 10-inch springform pan and dust with a little flour. Spoon in the cake batter and bake in the preheated oven for about 25 minutes. As soon as the cake is ready, unmold it onto a wire rack and leave to cool.

Meanwhile, make the custard sauce. Heat the milk with the lemon peel and remaining vanilla. In a bowl, beat the egg yolks with ¹/₄ cup sugar. Gradually stir in the hot, but not boiling, milk, then return the custard sauce to the saucepan you used for the milk and set over low heat. Stirring continuously, heat the sauce until thickened, without letting it boil, or it will curdle. As soon as it is ready, take

off the heat and leave to cool.

To prepare the strawberry sauce, purée 4 ounces of the strawberries with the remaining sugar at maximum speed, then place in a bowl. Now make the filling. Hull the remaining 5 ounces strawberries and cut into small pieces. Place in a bowl and macerate with 2 tablespoons of the liqueur. Meanwhile, whip the cream until very stiff, adding a spoonful of powdered sugar.

To assemble the tart, hollow out the center of the cake, reserving the crumbs. Moisten the cake with the remaining liqueur diluted with 3 tablespoons water, then fill it with the macerated strawberries, about one-third of the whipped cream and the cake crumbs. Level the surface to restore the cake to its original shape.

Put the remaining cream into a pastry bag with a fluted tip and pipe out 2 stripes to divide the cake into 2 semicircles. Fill the space between the stripes with the custard sauce and decorate with halved strawberries. Cover the semicircles with the sauce, and pipe rosettes of cream all around the edge. Place the tart on a serving plate and serve.

Strawberry Pillow

Mattonella Fragolina

To serve 6

3 eggs

¹/₂ cup sugar

a pinch of salt

¹/₂ teaspoon vanilla extract

1 cup all-purpose flour

butter and flour for the pan

3 tablespoons maraschino liqueur

1 cup whipping cream

1 tablespoon powdered sugar

10 ounces strawberries

6 tablespoons sugar

Preparation and cooking time:
about 1¹/₄ hours

First make a cake. (You can make it 4 or 5 days in advance and keep it wrapped in plastic wrap.) Preheat the oven to 350°F. Beat the eggs with the sugar and salt to a ribbon consistency. Stir in the vanilla, then fold in the flour delicately, working from bottom to top and vice-versa. Grease and flour a rectangular 12- x 5-inch cake pan and pour in the batter. Bake in the preheated oven for about 35 minutes. Check that the cake is baked by inserting a wooden skewer into the center. When it comes out dry, take the cake out of the oven and leave in the pan for 5 minutes, then turn it out onto a wire rack and leave to cool.

To assemble the pillow, split the sponge cake lengthwise and moisten both halves with the liqueur diluted with 3 tablespoons cold water. Whip the cream until stiff and sweeten with the powdered sugar.

Spoon about half the cream onto one cake rectangle. Hull, rinse, drain and slice the strawberries, then arrange two-thirds of them on top of the cream. Cover with the other cake rectangle.

Purée the remaining strawberries with the sugar to make a thick sauce. Fill a pastry bag with a fluted tip with the remaining whipped cream, and pipe

a border of cream swirls all around the edge of the dessert. Pour the sauce over the middle of the dessert to fill this border, transfer to a serving plate and serve immediately.

Strawberry Mousse

Turbante Rosa Fragola

To serve 8-10

2 tablespoons unflavored gelatin

a little almond oil

¹/₂ pound just-ripe strawberries

¹/₂ cup sugar

2¹/₄ cups whipping cream

4 tablespoons orange liqueur

2 tablespoons shredded coconut

10 equal-sized strawberries, with their stems, for decoration

fresh mint leaves, for decoration

Preparation and cooking time:
about 1 hour, plus overnight chilling

Soak the gelatin in cold water. Lightly oil a 4¹/₂-cup bowl with the almond oil. Hull the strawberries and rinse them quickly. Lay them out to dry on a double layer of paper towels. When they are completely dry, process them in a blender with the sugar, then pour the purée into a bowl.

Whip the cream until it is stiff, then gently fold it into the strawberry purée, mixing in with an up-and-down movement to prevent the cream from deflating.

Heat the liqueur in a small saucepan until it begins to simmer. Remove from the heat and stir in the gelatin until it has dissolved. Add the coconut to the strawberry mixture, then slowly pour in the liqueur and gelatin in a trickle. Mix constantly with an up-and-down folding movement.

Pour into the bowl, bang it gently, cover with plastic wrap and refrigerate overnight. Turn the mousse out onto a serving dish and decorate with the strawberries and the mint leaves. Serve at once.

Strawberry Tart *(left) and*
Strawberry Pillow *(above)*

Fruit Salad Tart

Crostata alla Macedonia

To serve 6

10 ounces frozen piecrust dough

1¼ cups milk

pared peel of 1 lemon

3 egg yolks

6 tablespoons sugar

¼ cup all-purpose flour

butter and flour for the pan and work surface

6 ounces peaches

3 ounces kiwifruit

1 large banana

2 ounces strawberries

1½ ounces bilberries

1½ ounces raspberries

2 pineapple rings

1 lemon

Preparation and cooking time: 1 hour, plus thawing

Thaw the dough. Meanwhile, prepare the filling. In a small saucepan, heat the milk with the well-washed and dried lemon peel. In a bowl, beat the egg yolks with the sugar and sifted flour, then gradually pour in the warm milk. Return the mixture to the pan, and cook, stirring continuously, until the custard sauce thickens. Do not let it boil. Take the custard sauce off the heat and leave to cool at room temperature, stirring occasionally to prevent a skin from forming.

Preheat the oven to 375°F. Lightly grease and flour an 8-inch tart pan. Flour the work surface and roll out the dough into a circle large enough to line the bottom and sides of the pan. Line the bottom with aluminum foil and fill with dried baking beans. Bake in the preheated oven for 30 minutes. Remove the beans and foil and leave the tart shell to cool on a wire rack.

Make the fruit salad only at the last moment, or the fruit will discolor and lose some of their juices. Peel and wash all the fruit, drain and dice or slice into

rounds, then place in a bowl. Cover with plastic wrap and refrigerate until ready to use, if you have to make it in advance.

When you are ready to serve, fill the tart with the custard sauce and decorate with the fruit.

Mixed Fruit Mélange

Fantasia di Frutta

To serve 2

3 firm, ripe mandarin oranges

2 kiwifruits

1 small banana

3 red and 3 green maraschino cherries

1 tablespoon sugar

juice of ½ lemon

2 tablespoons liqueur of your choice

Preparation time: about 30 minutes

Wash and dry the mandarins, then cut them in half crosswise. Use a grapefruit knife to loosen the flesh from the skin, without actually removing it. Peel the kiwifruits and slice them thinly into 16 to 18 slices. Cut the same number of slices from the banana and finally cut both the red and green cherries in half.

Arrange the 6 mandarin halves in the center of 2 small, oval-shaped dishes and decorate with the cherries. Put the slices of kiwifruit round the outside, topped with the banana slices. Leave to rest for a few minutes (do not place in the refrigerator).

Meanwhile, put the sugar in a bowl, add the strained lemon juice and stir until the sugar dissolves. Mix this cold syrup with the liqueur and stir again. Pour over the fruit and serve immediately.

Fresh Apricots

Composta di Albicocche

To serve 6

1¼ pounds firm, ripe apricots

⅓ cup apricot jam

1 tablespoon white rum

1 tablespoon apricot liqueur

grated peel of 1 lemon

1 lime for decoration

6 maraschino cherries

Preparation time: about 15 minutes, plus 1½ hours soaking

Remove the stems from the apricots and wipe them with a damp cloth. Halve them, remove the pits and slice them into a bowl.

Strain the jam, then dilute it with the rum and liqueur and add the grated lemon peel. Mix well and pour over the apricots, stirring carefully. Cover the bowl with plastic wrap and chill for at least 1½ hours, gently stirring from time to time.

Serve the apricots in 6 individual bowls. Garnish each one with 5 wafer-thin lime slices and 5 maraschino cherry slices. Serve at once.

Fruit Salad Flan

Summer Fruit Fantasy

Summer Fruit Fantasy

Macedonia Solare

To serve 6

1 large slice ripe watermelon, weighing about 1¹/₄ pounds

2 tablespoons white rum

a small bunch of black grapes

2 tablespoons sugar

2 tablespoons orange liqueur

3 large peaches (not too ripe)

juice of ¹/₂ lemon

fresh mint leaves for decoration

Preparation time: about 1¹/₄ hours

Using a melon baller, make small, equal-sized balls from the slice of watermelon, discarding any seeds. Place the melon balls in a bowl and sprinkle with the white rum. Cover the bowl with plastic wrap and refrigerate for about 30 minutes.

Wash and dry the grapes, and reserve the best ones. Place the grapes in a small bowl, sprinkle with 1 tablespoon of the sugar and the Cointreau, then set them aside to rest in a cool place for about 15 minutes.

Wash and dry the peaches, cut them into thin slices and drop them into a bowl. Sprinkle with the remaining sugar and the strained lemon juice. Mix gently, cover the bowl and leave in a cool place for about 15 minutes.

Before serving, arrange the fruit in circles on a large serving dish, decorated with leaves of fresh mint and the reserved grapes, and serve.

September Fruit Salad

Capriccio Settembrino

To serve 4

2 apples

juice of 1 lemon

¹/₄ cup sugar

1 peach

12 ounces Victoria plums

¹/₂ pound green grapes

3 tablespoons orange liqueur

Preparation time: about 30 minutes, plus 1 hour chilling

Peel and core the apples, cut into quarters and then dice them. As they are diced, drop them into a bowl containing the strained lemon juice. Add the sugar, then stir gently with a wooden spoon.

Remove the stems from the peach and the plums and wipe them with a damp cloth. Cut them in half and remove the pits, then dice them and add them to the apples in the bowl. Wipe the grapes with a damp cloth and remove stems and seeds if necessary. Cut the larger grapes in half. Add to the rest of the fruit. Mix well and pour the liqueur over.

Cover with plastic wrap and chill for at least 1 hour. Stir gently before serving.

Fruit Cup

Coppa di Frutta

To serve 4

¹/₂ pomegranate

2 tablespoons orange liqueur

20 green grapes

2 tablespoons sugar

juice of ¹/₂ lemon

4 oranges

Preparation time: about 40 minutes

Peel the pomegranate and place the segments in a bowl. Sprinkle with the liqueur and stir gently. Cover the bowl and place in a cool place. Leave the fruit to soak for about 15 minutes.

Wash and dry the grapes and cut each one lengthwise into 4 segments, taking care to remove the seeds. Place the segments in a bowl and dust with the sugar. Sprinkle with the lemon juice, stir and set aside in a cool place for a few minutes.

Peel the oranges, taking care to remove all the pith. Divide the oranges into segments and place in a serving bowl, squeezing any juice remaining in the peel over them. Add the pomegranate and grape segments, together with their juices, to the orange segments and stir well. Keep in the refrigerator until you are ready to serve this dessert.

September Fruit Salad *(above) and* ***Fruit Cup*** *(left)*

Zabaglione Trifle

Dolce al Cucchiaio

To serve 10-12

4 eggs, plus 3 extra yolks

³/₄ cup sugar, plus 1 extra tablespoon

¹/₂ teaspoon vanilla extract

1 cup all-purpose flour

salt

butter and flour for the pan and baking sheet

¹/₄ cup Marsala wine

3 apples

2 cups heavy cream

6 tablespoons maraschino liqueur

juice of 1 lemon

raspberries

Preparation and cooking time:
about 2 hours

First make a sponge. Preheat the oven to 375°F. Beat 3 eggs and ¹/₂ cup of the sugar together with the vanilla until light and fluffy. Sift in the flour and a pinch of salt and beat until the mixture makes a smooth batter.

Butter and flour an 8-inch cake pan. Spoon the batter in, then bake in the oven for about 35 minutes, or until the cake springs back when lightly pressed with a finger. Turn the cake out and leave to cool on a wire rack. Increase the oven temperature to 475°F.

Now prepare the zabaglione. Combine ¹/₄ cup of the sugar with the Marsala wine, the remaining egg and the egg yolks and a pinch of salt in a stainless-steel bowl. Stand the bowl in a bain-marie of warm water, place over very low heat and beat the eggs until they increase in volume and become creamy and thick. Remove from the bain-marie and leave to cool.

Core 2 of the apples, then peel and thinly slice them. Arrange on a greased baking sheet. Sprinkle with an extra tablespoon sugar, then cook in the hot oven for about 5 minutes. Whip the cream and fold about 1 cup into the prepared zabaglione. Dilute the liqueur with a little cold water.

Cut the cake into small slices, then brush them with the liqueur and arrange a few in the bottom of a bowl. Cover with half the zabaglione, and follow with alternate layers of apple, cake, apple and zabaglione. Level the surface smoothly.

Thinly slice the remaining apple, without peeling it. Dip the slices in lemon juice, then drain and arrange them around the edge of the trifle. Put the remaining whipped cream in a pastry bag with a ridged tip and pipe decoratively onto the trifle. Finish the decoration with raspberries, and keep in the refrigerator until you are ready to serve the trifle.

Little Orange Balls

Bignoline al Fior d'Arancio

To serve 8-10

2 cups all-purpose flour

¹/₂ teaspoon baking powder

¹/₄ cup sugar

2 tablespoons olive oil

1 tablespoon rum

grated peel of ¹/₂ lemon

a pinch of salt

2 eggs, plus 1 extra egg yolk

vegetable oil for greasing and frying

1 tablespoon orange-flower water

5 tablespoons honey

¹/₃ cup candied orange peel

10 blanched almonds

Preparation and cooking time:
about 2 hours

Sift the flour and baking powder together. Make a well in the center and add the sugar, olive oil, rum, lemon peel, salt, eggs and egg yolk. Fold the ingredients into the flour and combine to make a firm smooth paste. Divide into small balls about the size of a hazelnut, then place on a lightly oiled sheet of aluminum foil and leave to stand for 30 minutes.

Heat plenty of oil in a large deep-frying pan, then fry the balls a few at a time. When they are golden brown,

drain them well on paper towels.

Put the orange-flower water, and the honey into a large pan. Heat gently and stir until the ingredients have melted. Leave to cool and then add the candied orange peel, the chopped almonds and the fried balls. Stir well, then mound onto a serving dish and serve at once.

Mandarin Orange Trifle

Crema ai Mandarini

To serve 6-8

1 tablespoon unflavored gelatin

4 egg yolks

6 tablespoons sugar

a little vanilla sugar

1 teaspoon cornstarch

a pinch of salt

1 cup milk

2 cups heavy cream

2 ounces sliced pound cake

4 tablespoons Strega

1 slice canned pineapple

1 brandied fig

1 small can mandarin oranges

4 tablespoons orange marmalade

chocolate sprinkles

Preparation and cooking time:
about 1 hour, plus 2 hours chilling

Dissolve the gelatin in a little water. Place the egg yolks, sugar, vanilla sugar, cornstarch and salt in a saucepan and beat together until smooth. Dilute with the cold milk and half the cream, then bring to a boil, stirring with a small balloon whisk. Remove from the heat, stir in the gelatin, and leave to cool but not set, stirring frequently.

Cut the cake into ³/₄-inch cubes. Place in a large bowl or soufflé dish and soak with the Strega. When the custard sauce has cooled, whip the remaining cream until stiff and fold carefully into the custard. Spread the

custard over the cake pieces and refrigerate the bowl for at least 2 hours, or until the custard has set.

Arrange a well-drained pineapple ring and the brandied fig in the center, and mandarin sections all around, slightly overlapping. Warm the marmalade with a little water, strain it and use it to brush the fruit and the surface of the dessert. Decorate with chocolate sprinkles and serve at once.

Orange Bavarois

Bavarese all'Arancia

To serve 8

1 tablespoon unflavored gelatin

2¹/₂ cups milk

5 egg yolks

³/₄ cup sugar

3 oranges

¹/₂ teaspoon vanilla extract

3 tablespoons orange liqueur

2¹/₂ cups whipping cream

diced candied mixed fruit

mixed candied citrus fruit

Preparation time: about 1 hour, plus 12 hours chilling

Soak the gelatin in cold water while you heat the milk. In a bowl, beat the egg yolks with the sugar, then gradually stir in the hot, but not boiling, milk. Thoroughly wash and grate the peel of 2 oranges, and add to the custard sauce, together with the vanilla. Set over low heat and heat the custard sauce until thickened, stirring continuously, without letting it boil, or it will curdle. Take the sauce off the heat. Add the gelatin with the orange liqueur and stir well to dissolve the gelatin completely, then leave the custard sauce to cool at room temperature.

When the custard sauce has just begun to set, whip the cream very stiffly and fold it into the custard. Pour the mixture into a dampened 7¹/₂-cup mold and refrigerate for 12 hours.

Orange Bavarois

Just before serving the bavarois, pass the mold over the steam from a pan of boiling water, then invert it onto a plate. Decorate the dessert with the remaining whipped cream, using a pastry bag with a fluted tip. Pipe on stripes and rosettes, surround it with thin slices cut from the remaining orange, and finish with a little heap of candied fruit in the middle and thin slices of candied citrus fruit around the edge.

Vanilla Ice Cream

Gelato alla Vaniglia

To serve 6

2¹/₂ cups milk

³/₄ cup sugar

salt

1 small vanilla bean

5 egg yolks, plus 1 extra white

Preparation time: 30 minutes, plus freezing

Heat most of the milk in a saucepan with the sugar, salt and the vanilla bean until almost boiling. Remove from the heat and remove the bean.

Meanwhile, beat the egg yolks then add, little by little, first the reserved cold milk, then the hot, stirring constantly. When the ingredients are well blended, pour the mixture back into the saucepan and heat for about 2 minutes, stirring.

Pour the mixture into a bowl and let it cool, stirring occasionally. Pour it into an ice-cream maker, straining it through a fine strainer. Churn until the ice cream starts to become creamy. Beat the egg white with a pinch of salt and fold it into the ice-cream mixture; this helps to make the ice cream smooth and soft. Finish churning the ice cream, then transfer it to a freezerproof bowl and freeze until required.

Baked Peaches with Vanilla Ice Cream

Pesche al Forno con Gelato alla Vaniglia

To serve 8

4 large peaches, about 1³/₄ pounds

heaped ³/₄ cup sugar

2 tablespoons butter

2 tablespoons Amaretto liqueur

juice of ¹/₂ lemon

1³/₄ cups milk

4 coffee beans

1 vanilla bean

5 egg yolks

¹/₂ cup whipping cream

powdered sugar

Preparation time: about 40 minutes, plus freezing

Preheat the oven to 400°F. Rinse and dry the peaches, halve and pit them and arrange in a baking dish. Sprinkle on 3 tablespoons of the sugar, flakes of butter, the Amaretto liqueur and the lemon juice. Cover the dish with foil, then bake in the preheated oven for about 20 minutes.

Meanwhile, prepare the ice cream. Heat the milk with the coffee beans and vanilla bean. In a bowl, mix together the egg yolks and remaining sugar, then gradually strain in the hot, but not boiling, milk, pouring it through a fine strainer. Pour the custard back into the pan and heat very gently until thickened; do not let it boil.

Take the pan off the heat and leave the custard to cool before pouring it into an ice-cream maker. Churn until the ice cream becomes creamy, then stir in the lightly whipped cream and finish churning. Transfer the ice cream to a freezerproof bowl and freeze until required.

Scoop out balls of ice cream and arrange them among the cold, baked peaches. Dust with powdered sugar and serve.

Coconut Ice Cream with Candied Pineapple

Gelato al Cocco con Ananas Caramellato

To serve 6

¹/₄ cup milk

¹/₄ cup sugar, plus a little extra for the pineapple purée

¹/₄ cup heavy cream

1 teaspoon vanilla extract

²/₃ cup coconut milk

a glass of rum, plus a dash extra for flambéeing

Baked Peaches with Vanilla Ice Cream

1 large pineapple

butter

a pinch of cornstarch

black currants

Preparation time: about 40 minutes, plus freezing

To make the ice cream, heat, but do not boil, the milk with the sugar, cream and half the vanilla. Take the pan off the heat and add the coconut milk and the rum. Leave to cool, then pour the mixture into an ice-cream maker and churn according to the directions. As soon as the ice cream is creamy, transfer it to a freezerproof bowl and freeze until required.

Shortly before serving, peel and core the pineapple and cut 6 even slices from the middle of the fruit, about $\frac{1}{2}$ inch thick. Purée the remainder with $\frac{1}{2}$ cup cold water and a spoonful of sugar.

Strain the purée and set aside.

Dry the pineapple slices and brown them over high heat with a nut of butter, then remove them from the pan and flambé the cooking juices with a dash of rum. As soon as the alcohol has evaporated, add the cornstarch slaked with a drop of water and the reserved pineapple purée. Cook over a medium heat until the sauce has thickened, then turn off the heat, beat in a nut of butter and flavor with the remaining vanilla.

Arrange the pineapple slices and scoops of ice cream on a plate, pour the sauce all over and decorate with clusters of black currants.

Coconut Ice Cream with Candied Pineapple

Coffee Ice Cream

Gelato al Caffè

To serve 6

4 tablespoons ground coffee

2 tablespoons vanilla sugar

1³/₄ cups sugar

1 cup light cream

1 egg white

a pinch of salt

Preparation time: 30 minutes, plus chilling and freezing

In a small saucepan, bring 1¹/₂ cups water to a boil, pour in the coffee and, stirring constantly, simmer over very low heat until the foam has disappeared. Leave to infuse for about 15 minutes, so that the ground coffee sinks to the bottom of the saucepan; strain the liquid coffee into a bowl.

Add the vanilla sugar and the sugar and stir until the sugar dissolves, then leave to cool. At this point, stir in the cream and place in the refrigerator for at least 1 hour to cool completely.

Pour the mixture into an ice-cream maker. Add the egg white beaten to a froth with the salt, so that the ice cream will be smooth and soft. Churn according to the directions. Transfer to a freezerproof bowl and freeze until required.

Lemon Ice Cream with Strawberry Coulis

Gellato Rosato

To serve 4

2 pints lemon ice cream

¹/₂ pound fresh strawberries

3 tablespoons orange liqueur

2 tablespoons sugar

8 wafers

Preparation time: about 15 minutes, plus 2 hours soaking

Keep the ice cream in the freezer for at least 2 hours before preparation.

Meanwhile, rinse the strawberries, drain well and discard the hulls. Cut the strawberries into pieces and place them in a bowl. Pour in the orange liqueur and sprinkle with the sugar. Cover the bowl and leave to soak for a couple of hours.

Just before you are ready to serve, purée the strawberries with their syrup to form a smooth sauce. Remove the ice cream from the freezer and, using a scoop, place balls of the ice cream either in a large serving goblet or in individual glasses. Coat the ice cream with the strawberry sauce and serve with the wafers.

Lemon Ice Cream with Strawberry Coulis

Pistachio Ice Cream

Gelato al Pistacchio

To serve 6

²/₃ **cup shelled pistachio nuts**

a pinch of salt

1 cup sugar

2¹/₂ **cups milk**

1 vanilla bean

5 egg yolks

Preparation time: 30 minutes, plus freezing

Plunge the pistachio nuts into salted boiling water for 1 minute, then drain and shell them. Pound them in a mortar, adding 1 tablespoon of the sugar from time to time, until they are reduced to powder.

Heat most of the milk with the remaining sugar and the vanilla bean, then bring slowly to a boil, stirring occasionally with a wooden spoon. Remove from the heat and discard the vanilla bean.

Meanwhile, beat the egg yolks in a bowl with the powdered pistachio nuts, using a small balloon whisk to make a smooth mixture. Add first the reserved cold milk, then the hot, stirring constantly. When the ingredients are well blended, pour the mixture back into the saucepan and heat for about 2 minutes, stirring. Pour the mixture into a bowl and let it cool, stirring occasionally.

Pour the mixture into an ice-cream machine, straining it through a fine strainer, and churn according to the directions. When the ice cream is creamy, transfer to a freezerproof bowl and freeze until required.

Amaretto Ice Cream

Gelato all'Amaretto

To serve 6

2¹/₂ **cups milk**

1 vanilla bean

5 egg yolks

a pinch of salt

³/₄ **cup sugar**

4 ounces Amaretti macaroons

4 tablespoons Amaretto liqueur

Preparation and cooking time: 1¹/₂ hours, plus freezing

Heat the milk in a saucepan with the vanilla bean and bring slowly to a boil. Strain, remove from the heat and remove the bean. Leave to cool.

Meanwhile, beat the egg yolks with the salt and sugar until soft and frothy. Stir in the warm milk, pouring it in a trickle, then beat until well blended. Pour the mixture back into the saucepan, place over a very low heat and heat, stirring constantly, until the mixture is about to boil.

Remove from the heat and strain the liquid through a fine strainer, then leave to cool at room temperature, stirring occasionally. Add the finely crumbled Amaretti macaroons and Amaretto liqueur. Place in the refrigerator for about 1 hour, then pour the mixture into an ice cream-maker. Churn, following the directions. When the ice cream is creamy, transfer it to a freezerproof bowl and freeze until required.

Ice Cream Cake

Torta Gelato

To serve 8

5 cups milk

3 eggs, plus 4 extra yolks

2¹/₂ cups sugar

1 teaspoon vanilla extract

14 ounces peaches, peeled and pitted, plus extra for decorating

1 cup all-purpose flour

butter and flour for the cake pan

¹/₃ glass maraschino liqueur

¹/₂ cup cherry jam

2 peaches, sliced

1 cup whipping cream, whipped

1 banana, sliced

Preparation time: about 1 hour, plus freezing

1) To make the vanilla ice cream, heat 2¹/₂ cups of the milk. In a bowl, beat the 4 egg yolks with ³/₄ cup of the sugar and ¹/₄ teaspoon of the vanilla, then gradually pour in the hot milk. Return the custard to the pan and simmer over very low heat for a few minutes, stirring continuously. Do not let it boil.

2) Pour the custard into an ice-cream maker and churn according to the directions. When the ice cream is creamy, transfer it to a freezerproof bowl and freeze until required.

To make the peach ice cream, purée the peaches with the remaining milk and ¹/₂ cup of the sugar. Churn in the ice-cream maker, then freeze.

3) Now make a cake for the bottom. Preheat the oven to 350°F. Beat the eggs with the remaining sugar to a ribbon consistency. Stir in the remaining vanilla, then sift in the flour from a height and fold in. Grease and flour a round 9-inch cake pan and spoon in the cake batter. Bake in the preheated oven for about 35 minutes. Remove from the oven and leave to cool on a wire rack.

4) Blend the liqueur with the cherry jam and 2 tablespoons cold water. Split the cake horizontally into 3 layers and brush each with the jam mixture.

5) Line the base of a 9-inch springform cake pan with waxed paper. Line the edge with a ³/₄-inch strip of cake.

6) Fill the mold with half the peach ice cream, cover with peach slices, then make a layer of all the vanilla ice cream and finish with the remaining peach ice cream. Cover the top securely with thick foil and place the cake in the freezer.

To serve, remove the ice cream cake from the freezer and let it stand for 5-10 minutes. Remove the foil and unmold onto a serving plate, easing away the sides of the cake pan with a spatula, if necessary. Decorate with whipped cream and sliced banana and peaches.

1

2

3

4

5

6

Tricolor Ice Cream Tart

Torta Gelato Tricolore

To serve 8

¹/₂ cup fresh apricot pulp

2¹/₄ cups milk

2¹/₄ cups sugar

³/₄ cup whipping cream

4¹/₂ ounces raspberries

1 vanilla bean

3 eggs, plus 2 extra yolks

a pinch of salt

¹/₂ teaspoon vanilla extract

1 cup all-purpose flour

butter and flour for the baking sheet

fresh fruit for decoration

Preparation and cooking time: about 1 hour, plus freezing

The ice creams can be prepared a day in advance. For the apricot ice cream, blend the pulp with ²/₃ cup of the milk, ¹/₂ cup of the sugar and half the unwhipped cream for about 1 minute. Pour into an ice-cream maker and churn according to the directions. As soon as the ice cream is creamy, transfer it to a freezerproof bowl and place in the freezer. Make the raspberry ice cream in the same way, using the raspberries, ²/₃ cup of the milk, ¹/₂ cup of the sugar and 6 tablespoons of the

unwhipped cream, then freeze it.

To make the vanilla ice cream, heat the remaining milk with the vanilla bean. Meanwhile, mix the egg yolks with 6 tablespoons sugar. Gradually pour in the strained hot milk, then return the custard to the pan and cook until thickened, but do not boil. Leave the custard to cool, then pour it into an ice-cream maker and churn according to the directions.

As soon as it is ready, transfer it to a springform cake pan, cover with freezer foil and freeze until solid.

Spread the raspberry ice cream over the vanilla and then add the apricot ice cream. Level the surface. Re-cover and keep in the freezer until ready to serve.

To make a cake base, beat the eggs with the remaining sugar, salt and the vanilla until puffed up and light, then fold in the sifted flour. Spoon the batter into a greased 8¹/₂-inch jelly-roll pan lined with a sheet of greased and floured waxed paper, then bake in the preheated oven for about 15 minutes. Remove from the oven, peel the cake off the paper and, when it is cool, cut out a circle the same diameter as the springform pan. Unmold the ice cream on to the cake, garnish with slices of fresh fruit, then serve.

Nougat Ice Cream

Gelato al Torroncino

To serve 6

1 cup assorted candied fruit

¹/₄ cup maraschino liqueur

4 ounces Italian nougat (torrone)

2¹/₂ cups milk

1 vanilla bean

1 cup sugar

4 egg yolks

Preparation and cooking time:
1¹/₂ hours, plus freezing

Coarsely chop the candied fruit, of different colors and flavors, then place it in a small bowl and moisten it with the maraschino liqueur. Pound the nougat to a powder.

In a saucepan, heat most of the milk with the vanilla bean and the sugar. When the milk is hot and the sugar has dissolved, discard the vanilla bean.

Beat the egg yolks in a bowl, adding first the reserved cold milk, then the hot, pouring it in a trickle and stirring constantly. When all the ingredients are well mixed, pour them back into the saucepan and heat for a couple of minutes, stirring, without bringing it to a boil. Remove the saucepan from the heat and strain the mixture into a bowl. Let it cool, stirring occasionally, then leave it for at least 1 hour in the refrigerator.

Just before placing it in an ice-cream machine, mix in the candied fruit and the nougat. Churn according to the directions, then transfer to a freezerproof bowl and freeze until required.

Pear Ice Cream with Fruits of the Forest Sauce

Gelato di Pere con Salsa ai Frutti di Bosco

To serve 6

14 ounces pears

1 cup sugar

2¹/₄ cups milk

5 ounces bilberries

5 ounces raspberries

4 ounces black currants

6 tablespoons Grappa

langue de chat cookies

Preparation time: about 30 minutes, plus freezing and macerating

First make the ice cream. Peel and core the pears, then dice them and place in a blender or food processor. Add ³/₄ cup of the sugar and the milk and blend at maximum speed for 1 minute,

then pour the mixture into an ice-cream maker and churn according to the directions. When the ice cream is creamy, transfer it to a freezerproof bowl and freeze until required.

To make the sauce, rinse the fruit and drain well, then place them in a bowl with the remaining sugar and the grappa. Cover with plastic wrap and leave to macerate in the refrigerator for at least 6 hours.

When you are ready to serve the ice cream, scoop it into 6 appropriate coupes and pour the fruit sauce over. Finish with some _langue de chat_ cookies and serve immediately.

**Tricolour Ice Cream Tart** (left) and **Pear Ice Cream with Fruits of the Forest Sauce** (above)

Greedy Nests

Nidi Golosi

To serve 8

5 egg whites

3 cups sugar

a pinch of salt

¹/₂ teaspoon vanilla extract

butter and flour for the baking sheet

1³/₄ cups fresh peach pulp

2¹/₂ cups whipping cream

2¹/₂ cups milk

10 ounces raspberries

14 ounces peaches

7 ounces raspberries

fresh mint

Preparation and cooking time: about 3¹/₂ hours

First make the meringue. (This can be done several days in advance.) Preheat the oven to 140°F. Put the egg whites, 1¹/₂ cups of the sugar and the salt in a bowl and stand the bottom in a warm bain-marie. Beat until very firm, then add the vanilla. Put the meringue into a pastry bag with a fluted tip and pipe out 8 large nests onto a greased and floured baking sheet. Bake in the warm oven for about 3 hours, making sure that the nests are completely dry before removing them from the oven.

To make the peach ice cream, blend the peach pulp for 1 minute with ²/₃ cup of the unwhipped cream, half the sugar and 2 cups of the milk. Churn in an ice-cream maker according to the directions. As soon as the ice cream is creamy, transfer it to a freezerproof bowl and freeze. Make the raspberry ice cream in the same way, using the raspberries, ²/₃ cup unwhipped whipping cream, ³/₄ cup sugar and 2 cups milk.

To assemble the nests, whip the remaining whipping cream and divide it between the nests. Fill with balls of mixed ice cream and decorate with sliced peaches, raspberries and sprigs of mint.

Orange Sorbet

Sorbetto all'Arancia

To serve 8

juice of 6 or 7 juicy oranges (reserve the shells)

grated peel of 2 oranges

2 cups sugar, plus 2 tablespoons

1 egg white

a pinch of salt

2 tablespoons shelled pistachio nuts, blanched, skinned and chopped

cookies, to serve

Preparation time: about 30 minutes, plus freezing

Clean 8 orange shell halves, scraping out the internal membranes, then place them in the freezer. Strain the orange juice into a bowl. Mix in the grated peel and 2 cups sugar. Refrigerate the juice for about 2 hours, stirring frequently to dissolve all the sugar. Transfer the mixture to an ice-cream maker and churn according to the directions.

Meanwhile, beat the egg white with the salt until very firm, then fold in 2 tablespoons sugar. As soon as the orange juice mixture begins to firm up, stop churning for a moment and add half the beaten egg white (discard the remaining beaten egg white). Start the machine again and finish churning the sorbet. Place the sorbet in the freezer; the egg white will keep it soft.

Just before serving, take the orange shells out of the freezer and cut a sliver off the bottoms so that they stand firmly. Fill with the sorbet, sprinkle with chopped pistachios and serve with little cookies.

Greedy Nests (left), Orange Sorbet (above right) and Charlotte Meringue with Mandarin Sorbet (right)

Charlotte Meringue with Mandarin Sorbet

Charlotte Meringata al Sorbetto di Mandarino

To serve 8

²/₃ **cup fresh mandarin juice, plus the peel from the squeezed fruit**

1 cup sugar, plus 1 tablespoon extra

5 egg whites

1 sponge cake, about 7 inches round

6 tablespoons orange liqueur

10 ounces strawberries

¹/₄ **fresh pineapple, freshly diced**

a pinch of salt

Preparation and cooking time:
about 2 hours

Steep the mandarin peel overnight in the juice, ¹/₂ cup sugar and ²/₃ cups water.

Next day, strain the infusion and churn in an ice-cream maker, following the directions. As soon as it begins to solidify, add one-third of egg white beaten with the remaining 1 tablespoon sugar, and finish churning (discard the remaining beaten egg white). Transfer the sorbet to the freezer.

Slice the cake lengthwise into ¹/₂-inch slices. Cut 5 or 6 of the longest slices into rectangles as long as the diameter of your mold; halve them into equal triangles and arrange them like rays in the mold, the points converging in the center. Line the sides with some of the remaining slices, cutting off the excess.

Brush the lining cake slices with orange liqueur diluted with a little water. Fill the mold with the strawberries, pineapple and sorbet, alternating the layers with the remaining cake. Chill in the freezer for at least 4 hours.

Preheat the oven to 475°F. Just before serving, beat the remaining 4 egg whites with the salt until very firm, adding all the remaining sugar little by little.

Unmold the charlotte onto an ovenproof serving plate and cover it with this meringue, then bake in the hot oven for not more than 3 or 4 minutes. Serve immediately.

Ice Cream Cake with Forest Fruits

Biscotto Gelato ai Frutti di Bosco

To serve 8

4 eggs, plus 5 extra yolks

2¼ cups sugar

1¼ cups all-purpose flour

3 tablespoons cocoa powder

butter for greasing the pan

2½ cups milk

1 vanilla bean

1½ cups whipping cream

7 ounces mixed fruits of the forest

orange liqueur

Preparation and cooking time:
about 1 hour, plus freezing

1) Preheat the oven to 350°F. First make the cake. With an electric mixer, beat the eggs with ¾ cup of the sugar, then sift in the flour and cocoa from a height. Grease a jelly-roll pan, cover with a sheet of greased waxed paper and pour in the cake batter, leveling it with a spatula. Bake in the preheated oven for 8 minutes, then remove and invert the cake onto a cloth towel.

2) To make the ice cream, heat the milk with 1 cup of the sugar and the vanilla bean. Leave to cool, then strain. Add 1¼ cups of the cream, beat well and pour into an ice-cream maker. Churn according to the directions

3) Macerate half the fruit in 5 tablespooons orange liqueur. Place the rest in a saucepan with the remaining sugar, the egg yolks and 2 tablespoons orange liqueur. Beat together over medium heat until smooth and creamy. Leave to cool, then add the macerated fruit and ¼ cup whipped cream.

4) Trim the edges of the cake and use it to line the bottom and sides of a 3¾ cup mold. Brush lightly with orange liqueur.

5) Fill the mold with the ice cream, making a deep hollow in the center.

6) Fill up with the fruit and cream mixture, then cover the top with the sponge trimmings. Freeze for about 4 hours. Serve the ice cream cake with fresh fruit.

1

2

3

4

5

6

Winter Melon Sorbet

Sorbetto al Melone d'Inverno

To serve 4

¾ cup sugar

peel of 1 lemon, cut into strips

2 cups diced pale green melon flesh

vodka

1 egg white, lightly beaten

pomegranate seeds

lime slices

pale green winter melon slices

Preparation time: about 10 minutes, plus freezing

Boil the sugar with 1 cup water and the lemon peel for 2 minutes; strain this syrup and leave to cool.

Meanwhile, purée the melon pulp in a blender or food processor and add it to the cold syrup. Add a glass of vodka, then churn the mixture in an ice-cream maker, following the directions. As soon as the sorbet begins to thicken, add the egg white and finish churning the sorbet (about 20 minutes in total).

Transfer the chilled sorbet to a freezer-proof container and freeze. Serve scooped into balls like ice cream. Garnish with pomegranate seeds, lime slices and slivers of melon.

Iced Lemons with Lemon and Raspberry Sorbets

Cedri Ghiacciati

To serve 6

4 large lemons

2½ cups sugar

9 ounces fresh raspberries, plus a few for decoration

2 tablespoons rum

Preparation time: about 1 hour, plus overnight infusing

First make the lemon sorbet, beginning a day ahead. Thoroughly wash the 3 largest lemons and halve them vertically. Scrape out the pulp and juice into a bowl. Refrigerate the empty lemon shells. Mix together 1¼ cups of the sugar, 1¾ cups water and the pared peel of one-quarter lemon and leave in the refrigerator to infuse overnight.

Strain the infusion and the lemon juice and pulp, then pour into an ice-cream maker and churn according to the directions. Transfer the sorbet to a freezerproof bowl and freeze as soon as it is ready.

To make the raspberry sorbet, purée the raspberries with the remaining sugar, the rum and 1¾ cups water. Transfer to the ice-cream maker and churn according to the directions, then place the sorbet in the freezerproof bowl and freeze.

Just before serving, fill the lemon shells with a portion of both sorbets and decorate with fresh raspberries.

Coffee Sorbet in Pastry Baskets

Sorbetto al Caffè in Coupelle

To serve 8

2 cups sugar

1 cup very strong, black coffee

4 egg whites

¹/₂ cup all-purpose flour

¹/₄ cup butter, melted and cooled, plus extra for greasing baking sheet

¹/₂ cup powdered sugar

Preparation and cooking time: about 1 hour, plus freezing

First make the coffee sorbet. Boil 1¾ cups sugar with 1 cup water for 1 minute, then add the coffee to this syrup. Mix together and leave to cool. Pour the coffee syrup into an ice-cream maker and churn according to the directions.

Meanwhile, beat 2 of the egg whites with the remaining sugar until very firm. As soon as the sorbet begins to solidify, add ¹/₂ tablespoon of beaten egg white and finish churning. Transfer the sorbet to a freezerproof bowl and freeze.

To make the pastry baskets, preheat the oven to 425°F. In a bowl, combine the flour, cooled melted butter, powdered sugar and remaining unbeaten egg whites and mix with a small balloon whisk to make a soft paste. Brush a baking sheet with butter, cover with a sheet of parchment paper and grease this as well. Put on a small spoonful of paste, flatten it with the back of a spoon to make a very thin disk, about 6 inches across. Make at least 7 more disks in this way, spacing them well apart as they will spread during baking.

Bake in the hot oven for a few minutes, until they are pale in the center, but browned at the edges. Lift them off the paper with a spatula (they should be soft and malleable), then mold them into baskets over the bottom of an up-turned cup. Lift off the baskets when they are cool and firm.

Just before serving, fill the baskets with scoops of the sorbet and immediately take the dessert to the table.

Iced Lemons with Lemon and Raspberry Sorbets (left) *and Coffee Sorbet in Pastry Baskets* (below)

Pastry Baskets with Ice Cream and Rhubarb Compote

Coupelle Congelato e Composta Dirabarbo

To serve 6

¹/₂ cup all-purpose flour

2 egg whites

¹/₂ cup powdered sugar

¹/₄ cup butter, melted and cooled, plus extra for greasing

18 ounces rhubarb

1 apple

2 tablespoons butter

2 tablespoons sugar

vanilla ice cream, to serve

fresh mint, to decorate

Preparation and cooking time: about 1 hour

First make the pastry baskets. (The baskets can be prepared a day in advance and kept in a cool, dry place.) Preheat the oven to 400°F. In a bowl, mix the flour with the unbeaten egg whites, the sugar and cool melted butter. Stir very gently, then place a spoonful of the mixture on a greased baking sheet lined with a sheet of greased parchment paper. Flatten the little heap with the back of a spoon to make a thin 4-inch disk. Make at least 5 more disks in the same way, spacing them well apart.

Bake in the hot oven for 3 to 4 minutes, until the disks are browned at the edges but still pale in the centers. Carefully lift them off the baking sheet and, while they are still malleable, mold them over the bottom of an up-turned cup or glass to make basket shapes. Make at least 6 baskets.

Trim the rhubarb and peel away the tough fibers with a potato peeler, then cut into chunks. Cut the apple into wedges. Heat the butter until it is foaming, then brown the rhubarb and apple over high heat. Sprinkle with the

Pastry Baskets with Ice Cream and Rhubarb Compote and Pineapple Sorbet in Strawberry Sauce

sugar and cook until well coated.

Place 2 scoops of ice cream in each pastry basket, decorate with fresh mint leaves and serve on individual plates accompanied by the rhubarb compote.

Pineapple Sorbet in Strawberry and Rabspberry Sauce

Sorbetto di Ananas Affogato

To serve 6

2 cups peeled pineapple pieces, plus 2 large rings for decoration

2³/₄ cups sugar

1 egg white

7 ounces strawberries

4 ounces raspberries

2 tablespoons orange liqueur

Preparation time: about 30 minutes, plus freezing

To make the sorbet, purée the pineapple with 1¹/₂ cups of the sugar and 1¹/₂ cups water. Transfer to an ice-cream maker and churn according to the directions. When the sorbet starts to become firm and thick, add 1 tablespoon of stiffly beaten egg white (discard the remaining beaten egg white) and finish churning. Transfer the sorbet to a freezerproof bowl and freeze until ready to serve.

To make the sauce, purée the strawberries and raspberries with the remaining sugar, the orange liqueur and 6 tablespoons cold water.

Scoop out small balls of sorbet with an ice-cream scoop and place in serving bowls. Add 2 pineapple wedges cut from the rings to each bowl and smother with the fruit sauce.

Strawberry Ice Cream with Meringues

Gelata alla Meringa

To serve 6

¹/₂ pound strawberries

2³/₄ cups sugar

2¹/₄ cups milk

4 egg whites

¹/₄ teaspoon vanilla extract

butter for greasing

vanilla-flavored sauce

Preparation and cooking time: about 40 minutes, plus freezing the ice cream and baking the meringues

First make the ice cream. (This can be done several days in advance.) Hull, rinse and thoroughly drain the strawberries, then place them in the goblet of a blender with ³/₄ cup of the sugar and the milk. Blend on full power for 2 minutes, then transfer to an ice-cream maker and churn following the directions. When the ice cream is creamy, transfer it to a freezerproof bowl and freeze

You can also prepare the meringues in advance. Preheat the oven to 300°F. Put the egg whites, the remaining sugar and vanilla in a bowl. Stand the bowl in a pan containing 2 fingers of warm water, place over very low heat and beat the egg whites until very stiff.

Place the meringue in a pastry bag fitted with a plain tip. Grease a baking sheet, then pipe walnut-sized meringues onto it, spaced well apart. Bake in the preheated oven for about 3 hours, until the meringues are firm and crisp; they should be white and perfectly dry. If they begin to brown, prop the oven door open a little.

To serve, place 3 or 4 scoops of ice cream in each dish, together with 3 or 4 meringues. Serve with vanilla-flavored custard sauce.

Strawberry Ice Cream with Meringues

Panettone with Chocolate Mousse

Panettone con Mousse di Cioccolato

To serve 8-10

12 ounces semisweet chocolate

¹/₄ cup milk

³/₄ cup orange liqueur

2 eggs, separated, plus 1 extra yolk

1 cup whipping cream

1 x 2¹/₄-pound panettone

Preparation and cooking time:
about 40 minutes, plus freezing

To make the mousse, break up the chocolate and place it in a heatproof bowl. Add the milk and ¹/₄ cup of the liqueur and melt in a bain-marie. Off the heat, beat in the 3 egg yolks. Beat the egg whites until very stiff. Whip the cream until very firm.

Up-turn the panettone on the work surface. Make an incision 1¹/₂ inches from the edge and cut all around and three-quarters of the way down the cake (about 4 inches from the bottom) to remove the inside. Using a long knife with a flexible blade, gradually cut into the vertical incision. Holding

the knife handle firmly, rotate the blade to release the bottom of the soft inside and to remove it all in one piece.

Divide the inside of the panettone into 4 equal circles. Dilute remaining liqueur with a little cold water and liberally brush the inside of the panettone and the circles with this mixture.

Keeping the panettone upside-down, fill with one-quarter of the mousse. Cover with a circle, then with another layer of mousse, and continue to make layers in this way, finishing with the circle from the bottom of the panettone. Turn it the right way up and freeze for at least 2 hours before serving.

Little Pastry Shells with Chocolate Mousse

Coupelle con Mousse al Cioccolato

To make 8-10

¹/₂ cup butter, plus extra for greasing the baking sheet

4 egg whites

1 cup powdered sugar

1 cup all-purpose flour, plus extra for the baking sheet

1 teaspoon vanilla extract

10 ounces semisweet chocolate

¹/₄ cup rum

1 cup heavy cream

1 cup milk

2 egg yolks

6 tablespoons sugar

¹/₂ tablespoon all-purpose flour

Preparation and cooking time:
about 1 hour 40 minutes, plus chilling

First make the pastry shells. (You can do this the day before if you keep them in a cool, dry place.) Preheat the oven to 400°F.

Melt the butter without browning it, then set aside to cool. In a bowl, mix together the unbeaten egg whites with the powdered sugar, flour, half the vanilla and the cooled melted butter to make a soft paste.

Butter and flour a baking sheet. Place 1 tablespoon of the mixture on it, flattening it out with the back of a spoon to make a very thin disk 6 to 6¹/₂ inches in diameter. Place the baking sheet in the hot oven for about 4 minutes. Remove; the disk should be soft and pale in the center and lightly browned at the edges. Lift off with a spatula and mold it around the bottom of an up-turned cup. Leave to cool, then unmold. Repeat the procedure until all the paste is used up. (You should end up with 8 to 10 pastry shells.)

To make the mousse, break up the chocolate and place in a bowl with the rum. Stand the bowl in a pan with 2 fingers of warm water, place over very low heat and melt the chocolate, stirring frequently and gently. Leave to cool. Whip the cream very stiffly. Fold it gently into the cooled chocolate. Refrigerate for about 2 hours.

Finally, prepare the sauce. Heat the milk and, meanwhile, mix the egg yolks with the sugar, remaining vanilla and flour. Stir in the hot milk. Pour the mixture back into the pan and heat over very low heat, stirring continuously; do not let it boil. Turn off the heat and leave the custard sauce to cool.

Just before serving, divide the mousse and vanilla custard sauce equally between the pastry shells.

Chocolate Jelly Roll

Biscotto Arrotolato al Cioccolato

To serve 8

2 eggs, plus 2 extra yolks

6 tablespoons sugar

³/₄ cup all-purpose flour

butter and flour for greasing

6 tablespoons maraschino liqueur

7 ounces semisweet chocolate

1 cup mascarpone cheese

powdered sugar and cocoa powder, for dusting

Preparation and cooking time:
about 45 minutes, plus chilling

Preheat the oven to 375°F. Using an electric mixer, beat the eggs with the sugar until light and fluffy. Sift in the flour from a height. Line a 16- x 13¹/₂-inch jelly-roll tin with waxed paper and grease and flour the paper. Spoon in the cake batter, and level the surface well with a small spatula.

Bake the cake in the preheated oven for about 15 minutes. Remove from the oven and invert onto a scrupulously clean cloth towel. Roll up in the cloth and leave to cool.

Dilute the maraschino liqueur with 2 tablespoons cold water. Break up the chocolate and melt it in a bain-marie. When it has melted and is just warm, mix it with the eggs and mascarpone cheese, mixing the mixture with a

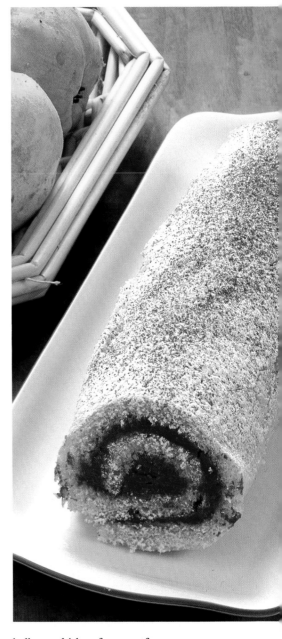

balloon whisk to form a soft cream. Refrigerate for 20 minutes to firm up slightly.

Unroll the cake. Moisten with the maraschino mixture and spread with the cream. Roll up again, using the cloth to help you. Wrap the jelly roll in plastic wrap and refrigerate for about 1 hour.

Just before serving, take the jelly roll out of the refrigerator, place on a serving plate and sift on a dusting of powdered sugar and cocoa.

Panettone with Chocolate Mousse (left) and Chocolate Jelly Roll (above)

Pistachio and Hazelnut Charlotte

Charlotte di Pistacchio e Nocciole

To serve 12

2 eggs, plus 3 extra yolks

³/₄ cup sugar, plus 1 tablespoon

¹/₂ teaspoon vanilla extract

³/₄ cup all-purpose flour, plus extra for the pan

finely grated peel of ¹/₂ lemon

²/₃ cup hazelnuts, toasted and skinned

2 ounces semisweet chocolate

1 cup heavy cream

3 tablespoons unflavored gelatin

1 cup milk

2 teaspoons cornstarch

²/₃ cup shelled pistachios, blanched and skinned

Preparation and cooking time:
about 1³/₄ hours, plus 6 hours chilling

Preheat the oven to 425°F. Beat the whole eggs, sugar and vanilla together until light and fluffy. Sift the flour with the grated lemon peel and fold delicately into the egg mixture.

Butter and flour a 9-inch long jelly-roll pan and line with waxed paper. Butter and flour the paper. Pour in the cake batter and level the surface. Bake for about 10 minutes. Turn out onto a cloth towel and set aside.

Grind the hazelnuts finely with 1 tablespoon sugar in a food processor to make a paste. Break the chocolate into pieces and place it in a bowl with ¹/₄ cup of the unwhipped cream and the hazelnut paste. Set the bowl in a pan with 2 fingers of water and melt the chocolate over very low heat.

Soften the gelatin in cold water. Heat the milk. Beat the 3 egg yolks with the remaining sugar and the cornstarch. Add the hot milk and stir in the gelatin, then set over very low heat and heat, stirring continuously; do not let it boil.

Divide the cream into 4 equal parts; add the chocolate mixture to one-quarter and the pistachios to another quarter. Blend the latter until smooth. Whip all the remaining cream and fold two-thirds of this into the pistachio cream. Chill in the refrigerator for about 20 minutes.

To assemble the charlotte, line a loose-bottomed round cake tin, 10 inches wide and 3¹/₂ inches deep, with some of the jelly roll. Fold the remaining whipped cream into the chocolate cream. Take the pistachio cream out of the refrigerator (it should have begun to set) and pour it into the pan. Spread the chocolate cream on top. Cover with slices of cake. Chill in the refrigerator for about 6 hours. Unmold and serve.

Chocolate and Pistachio Baskets

Coupelle al Cioccolata e Pistacchio

To make 12

³/₄ cup all-purpose flour

2 eggs, separated

¹/₂ cup powdered sugar

¹/₄ cup butter, melted and cooled

1 cup milk

6 tablespoons sugar

¹/₂ teaspoon vanilla extract

¹/₃ cup pistachios, shelled, peeled and finely chipped, plus a few whole pistachios for decoration

¹/₃ cup blanched almonds, finely chopped

4 ounces semisweet chocolate

Preparation and cooking time:
about 1 hour 20 minutes

until the chocolate melts, then add the Amaretto liqueur.

Remove the bowl from the bain-marie and leave the mixture to cool, then beat it until dense but still malleable. (Place the mixture in the refrigerator from time to time during this procedure.)

When the mixture is dense, chill it in the refrigerator for 30 minutes, then, with the aid of a spoon, divide it into 25 equal pieces. Roll each piece liberally in cocoa powder to make small balls (truffles). Place in paper candy cases and decorate each truffle with a hazelnut. Keep refrigerated until ready to serve.

*Pistachio and Hazelnut Charlotte (opposite), **Chocolate and Pistachio Baskets** (left) and **Hazelnut Truffles** (below)*

First prepare the baskets. (This can be done the day before; keep them in a cool, dry place.) Preheat the oven to 400°F. In a bowl, beat ½ cup of the flour with the egg whites, powdered sugar and cooled melted butter. Line a baking sheet with a sheet of parchment paper. Put on 1 tablespoon of the mixture and flatten it with the back of the spoon to make a thin 3½-inch circle. Add 2 more circles. Bake in the preheated oven for 3 to 4 minutes, until lightly browned at the edges and pale in the center. Remove from the oven and, while still warm, mold one inside a coffee cup. The dough will harden as it cools and can be formed into a basket. Make 12 baskets this way.

To make the pastry cream, heat the milk without letting it boil. Mix the egg yolks with the sugar and remaining flour, then pour in the hot milk in a steady stream. Return the mixture to the pan, set over a medium heat and simmer for 4 to 5 minutes, stirring continuously, to prevent lumps from forming. Take off the heat and stir in the vanilla. Leave to cool, then add the chopped pistachios and almonds.

Just before serving, coarsely chop the chocolate and melt it in a bain-marie. Brush it lavishly over the insides

of the baskets. Leave to harden, then place the pistachio filling in a pastry bag with a plain tip and fill up the baskets. Garnish with whole pistachios and serve.

Hazelnut Truffles

Tartufi alla Nocciola

To make 25

7 ounces semisweet chocolate

⅓ cup hazelnuts, shelled, toasted and finely chopped, plus 25 whole nuts for decoration

½ cup whipping cream

3 tablespoons Amaretto liqueur

cocoa powder

Preparation time: about 1 hour, plus chilling

Break up the chocolate and place in a bowl with the chopped hazelnuts and unwhipped cream. Stand the bowl in a bain-marie and set over medium heat

Chestnut and Chocolate Roll

"Salame" di Castagne e Cioccolato

To serve 12

10 tablespoons butter, softened

1 cup powdered sugar

³/₄ cup cocoa powder

4 tablespoons Amaretto liqueur

6-7 Amaretti macaroons

2 cups chestnut purée

chocolate sprinkles

a little whipping cream

Preparation and cooking time:
about 40 minutes, plus 3 to 4 hours chilling

Beat the butter in a bowl with a wooden spoon until light and frothy. Sift in the powdered sugar and the cocoa and mix in half the Amaretto liqueur. Grind the macaroons almost to a powder and add them, together with the chestnut paste and the remaining liqueur, reserving 1 teaspoon. Blend all the ingredients together smoothly.

Pour the reserved teaspoon of liqueur, diluted with 2 tablespoons of cold water, onto a sheet of aluminum foil. Spread the chestnut mixture on the foil and roll it up evenly and tightly. Seal the ends and refrigerate for 3 to 4 hours.

Just before serving, take the roll out of the refrigerator and remove the foil. Slice with a very sharp knife dipped in a bowl of hot water. Decorate, if you like, with a stripe of chocolate sprinkles and serve with whipped cream.

Rich Chocolate Cake

Torta "Gianfranco"

To serve 10

a little butter and flour for the pan

3 eggs, plus 2 extra yolks

2¹/₄ cups sugar

a pinch of salt

2 tablespoons vanilla sugar

10 ounces semisweet chocolate

1 cup all-purpose flour

¹/₂ cup potato flour

3 tablespoons cocoa powder

1 heaped teaspoon baking powder

²/₃ cup milk

1³/₄ cups whipping cream

¹/₃ cup slivered almonds

Preparation and cooking time:
about 1³/₄ hours, plus 4-5 hours chilling

Butter a 10-inch round cake pan and sprinkle it with flour. Beat the whole eggs briskly with ³/₄ cup of the sugar, the salt and the vanilla sugar until they form soft peaks.

Preheat the oven to 350°F. Melt 3 ounces of the chocolate over low heat and leave to cool. Mix all but 1 tablespoon of the flour with the potato flour, cocoa powder and the baking powder, then add to the egg mixture, carefully folding in with a wooden spoon. Fold in the melted chocolate and pour the batter into the prepared pan. Bake in the oven for about 30 minutes.

Meanwhile, beat the egg yolks with the remaining 1 tablespoon of flour, the sugar and a pinch of salt. Gradually add the milk and bring to a boil, stirring constantly. Remove the pan from the heat and leave to cool, stirring from time to time.

Cut 4 ounces of the chocolate into small pieces, then melt them over low heat. Add the melted chocolate to the mixture, stirring vigorously. Leave to cool.

Turn the cake out onto a wire rack. Whip the cream until stiff, then fold it into the chocolate mixture. Cut the cake into 3 layers and sandwich together with two-thirds of the chocolate mixture. Frost the top and sides of cake with some of the chocolate mixture and sprinkle with the remainder of the chocolate, grated. Pipe rosettes of chocolate mixture on the cake and decorate with slivered almonds. Refrigerate and serve within 4 or 5 hours.

Little Chocolate Puddings

Budinetti al Cioccolato

To make 8

4 eggs, plus 4 extra yolks

5 ounces semisweet chocolate

1³/₄ cups milk

1 cup whipping cream

1¹/₂ cups sugar, plus 2 tablespoons

2 oranges

3 tablespoons heavy cream

Preparation and cooking time:
about 1 hour, plus at least 6 hours
chilling

Preheat the oven to 375°F. Break the
chocolate into pieces and heat it with
the milk and cream until melted.

In a bowl, beat the eggs and yolks
lightly with ³/₄ cup of sugar. Gradually
pour the milk mixture onto the eggs,
stirring well.

Divide the mixture between 8
crème caramel molds or ramekins,
stand in a bain-marie filled with hot,
but not boiling, water and cook in the
oven for about 50 minutes. Leave to
cool, then place in the refrigerator and
chill for at least another 6 hours.

Pare off the orange peels and
squeeze the oranges. Measure the juice;
you should have ²/₃ cup; squeeze
another orange if necessary. In a small
saucepan, bring the juice to a boil with
2 tablespoons sugar and ²/₃ cup water.
Add a few strands of orange peel and
boil until you obtain a light syrup. Stir
in the cream and leave to cool.

In another saucepan, boil the
remaining peel with the remaining
³/₄ cup sugar and a very little water. Boil
until the water has evaporated and the
sugar has caramelized the peel.

Unmold the chocolate puddings
onto serving plates, pour the cold
orange syrup over and top with a little
heap of peel. Serve immediately.

egg lengthwise, to make 2 empty shells.

Sprinkle the ladyfingers with the
maraschino liqueur, then dip them into
the caramel to coat them. Whip the
cream until very stiff. Break up the
ladyfingers and put 3 in each egg shell,
alternating them with about half the
cream.

Put the remaining cream in a pastry
bag with a fluted tip and fill the shells
with rosettes of cream. Decorate with

grated chocolate and refrigerate until
ready to serve.

Chestnut and Chocolate Roll
(opposite), *Little Chocolate*
Puddings (above) **and** *Caramel-*
filled Easter Egg (below)

Caramel-filled Easter Egg

Uovo Pasquale al Caramello

To serve 4

³/₄ **cup sugar**

1 x 5-ounce hollow chocolate egg

6 ladyfingers

maraschino liqueur

1³/₄ **cups whipping cream**

grated chocolate, for decoration

Preparation time: about 30 minutes

Put the sugar in a saucepan with 4
tablespoons cold water, set over
medium heat and boil to a golden
caramel.

Meanwhile, heat a long-bladed
knife and use it to halve the chocolate

Zabaglione Dessert

Chiaroscuro allo Zabaione

To serve 4-6

3 eggs

¼ cup sugar

8 tablespoons dry Marsala wine

2 tablespoons golden raisins

1¼ cups whipping cream

12 chocolate-covered cookies

Preparation and cooking time:
about 30 minutes

Separate the eggs, placing the yolks in a saucepan with the sugar. Stir with a wooden spoon until pale and frothy, then stir in 6 tablespoons of the Marsala wine, one at a time. Heat the mixture in a double boiler, beating constantly with a small balloon whisk until it thickens. Leave to cool.

Meanwhile, soak the golden raisins for 15 minutes in warm water. When the zabaglione is cool, whip the cream and carefully stir in 3 tablespoons of it. Refrigerate the rest of the cream until it is required for decoration. Drain the golden raisins thoroughly and stir these in, too. Then spoon the mixture into a deep, square dish, distributing it evenly.

Pour 2 tablespoons of the Marsala wine into a soup bowl and add 2 tablespoons of water. Briefly dip the cookies in the mixture, keeping the chocolate-coated sides uppermost as you dip. Arrange the cookies diagonally on top of the zabaglione as you proceed, alternating the chocolate sides with the plain. Cut the cookies to fit the dish without leaving any gaps.

Put the remaining whipped cream into a pastry bag with a fluted, round tip and make a decorative border of swirls around the cookies. Refrigerate until serving time.

Zabaglione Dessert (top), Chocolate and Amaretti-Cream Cups (right) and Caramelized Chocolate Pillow (far right)

Chocolate and Amaretti-Cream Cups

Crema in Tazza al Cioccolato e Amaretti

To serve 8

$^1/_2$ tablespoon unflavored gelatin

5 egg yolks

1$^3/_4$ cups powdered sugar

2$^1/_4$ cups milk

7 ounces semisweet chocolate, chopped

4 ounces Amaretti macaroons

$^1/_2$ cup whipping cream, whipped

candied cherries

wafer curls, to decorate

Preparation and cooking time:
about 30 minutes, plus chilling

Soak the gelatin in a little cold water. In a bowl, beat the egg yolks with the powdered sugar, then gradually pour in the cold milk. Pour the mixture into a saucepan and add the chopped chocolate. Heat the custard sauce over a medium heat just until the chocolate melts; do not let it boil.

Crush the macaroons in a food processor, and add to the custard sauce with the dissolved gelatin. Take the pan off the heat and stir the custard sauce for another couple of seconds, then divide it between 8 cups and leave to cool before refrigerating for at least 2 hours.

Just before serving, decorate each cup with a rosette of whipped cream, a candied cherry and a couple of wafer curls.

Caramelized Chocolate Pillow

Mattonella al Cioccolato Caramellata

To serve 8

6 eggs, plus 3 extra yolks

2 cups sugar

a pinch of salt

$^1/_2$ teaspoon vanilla extract

1 cup all-purpose flour

butter and flour for the cake pan

5 ounces semisweet chocolate

5 ounces mixed candied fruit, plus extra candied cherries for decoration

1$^1/_4$ cups milk

1$^3/_4$ cups whipping cream

cocoa powder for dusting

Preparation and cooking time:
about 4 hours, plus 2$^1/_2$ hours chilling

First make a sponge cake. (This can be done several days in advance; wrap in plastic wrap and keep in a cool place until needed.) Preheat the oven to 350°F. With an electric mixer, beat 3 whole eggs and $^1/_2$ cup of the sugar with the salt to a ribbon consistency. Stir in the vanilla, then sift in the flour from a height, folding it in with a wooden spoon from bottom to top and vice versa. Grease and flour an 8$^1/_2$-inch cake pan and spoon in the cake batter. Bake in the preheated oven for about 35 minutes. To check if the cake is

baked, insert a skewer into the center; if it comes out dry, the cake is ready. Remove from the oven, unmold onto a wire rack and leave to cool.

Just before assembling the dessert, pour $^3/_4$ cup of the remaining sugar into a flameproof rectangular bread pan. Place on the heat until the sugar dissolves and caramelizes the base and sides of the pan. Take off the heat and leave the caramel to cool.

Meanwhile, preheat the oven to 375°F. Slice the cake, scrape the chocolate into slivers and finely dice the fruit. Beat the remaining eggs, 3 yolks and remaining sugar together, then add the milk.

Make alternating layers of cake, chocolate and fruit in the caramelized mold. Pour the egg mixture over, making sure that it fills the spaces between the layers. Place the mold in a roasting pan filled with 2 fingers of water and bake the dessert in this bain-marie for 2$^1/_2$ hours in the preheated oven. Remove from the oven and leave to cool.

Just before serving, whip the cream and put it in a pastry bag with a star tip. Unmold the dessert onto a serving plate and decorate with whirls of cream, candied cherries and a dusting of cocoa.

Chocolate Bavarois

Bavarese al Cioccolato

To serve 10

1 tablespoon unflavored gelatin

1 cup milk

3 egg yolks

1½ cups sugar

2½ cups whipping cream

5 ounces mixed candied fruits

kirsch

7 ounces semisweet chocolate

1½ tablespoons powdered sugar

11 ladyfingers

Preparation time: 1 hour, plus 12 hours chilling

Soak the gelatin in a little cold water and bring the milk to a boil. Meanwhile, put the egg yolks and sugar in a saucepan and mix together, then gradually pour in the hot milk, stirring very carefully. Immediately place the pan on the heat, add the gelatin and stir in, mixing continuously. When steam begins to rise from the custard sauce, take the pan off the heat and leave to cool. (To speed up the process, immerse the pan in cold water.) Refrigerate the cool custard.

Meanwhile, whip 1¼ cups of the cream very stiffly and finely chop the candied fruits, then steep them in kirsch. As soon as the custard sauce in the refrigerator begins to set (it should be gelatinous but not too firm, or it will be difficult to mix), remove it from the refrigerator and stir in the fruit, then the kirsch, then the whipped cream, folding it in extremely lightly. Transfer the mixture into a bavarois mold dampened with cold water and drained, level the surface well and chill in the refrigerator for at least 12 hours.

Decorate the bavarois shortly before serving. Grate and melt 5 ounces of the chocolate in a bowl set in a bain-marie of boiling water, stirring occasionally. Spread out the ladyfingers on a tray. When the chocolate is melted and smooth, spoon it over the ladyfingers, coating the top surfaces. Whip the remaining cream very stiffly and fold in the powdered sugar.

Unmold the bavarois onto a round serving plate and arrange the ladyfingers around the sides, spacing them evenly, with the chocolate sides outward.

Put the whipped cream in a pastry bag with a fluted tip and decorate the bavarois with stripes of cream between the ladyfingers and rosettes on the top of the ends. Grate the remaining chocolate and sprinkle it over the center of the bavarois, then serve.

Chocolate-glazed Cookies

Biscottini Glassati al Cioccolato

To serve 6

¾ cup butter, diced

2¼ cups all-purpose flour

⅓ cup shredded coconut

½ cup sugar

⅓ cup blanched almonds, finely chopped with ⅓ cup shelled hazelnuts

1 egg

a large pinch of salt

into a long sausage shape and cut into slices. Flatten these into thin wafers. Arrange on a baking sheet lined with waxed paper and bake in the hot oven for 13 minutes. Remove the cookies from the oven and leave to cool.

Break up the chocolate and melt it in a bain-marie, then brush it liberally over one side of each cookie. Place them, chocolate sides up, on a sheet of paper towels to set. As soon as the chocolate has dried completely, sprinkle the cookies with powdered sugar.

a small pinch of ground cinnamon

5 ounces semisweet chocolate

powdered sugar

Preparation and cooking time:
about 1 hour

Preheat the oven to 400°F. Using your fingertips, rub the butter with the flour until they resemble a mound of bread crumbs. Place on the work surface, make a well in the center and add the coconut, sugar, chopped almonds and hazelnuts, the egg, salt and the cinnamon. Knead to a dough, then roll

Coronets of Choux Puffs

Coroncine di Bignè

To serve 8

1³/₄ cups all-purpose flour

10 tablespoons butter, plus extra for greasing

salt

5 eggs

4¹/₂ ounces semisweet chocolate

¹/₄ cup crème de cacao liqueur

1³/₄ cups whipping cream, plus a little extra for decoration

³/₄ cup sugar, plus 4-5 tablespoons extra for the sauce

1¹/₂ cups ready-to-eat dried apricots

2 ounces raspberries

orange liqueur

Preparation and cooking time:
about 2 hours

Make the choux puffs following the directions on page 16 for Profiteroles in Spun Caramel, using the flour, ¹/₂ cup of the butter, a pinch of salt and the 5 whole eggs, beating them in one at a time. You should make about 40 puffs. You can make these a day in advance if it is more convenient.

Shortly before serving, prepare the filling. Break up the chocolate and melt it in a bain-marie with the crème de cacao. Meanwhile, whip the cream and stir it into the melted chocolate, stirring continuously. Refrigerate the mixture for 20 minutes.

Make an incision in the bottom of each choux puff, then fill them with the chocolate mixture. Arrange 5 puffs in a coronet on 8 serving plates.

Make a caramel with ³/₄ cup sugar and one-third of a glass of water, then pour the caramel over the choux puffs.

Slowly heat 4 to 5 tablespoons sugar with the remaining butter to make a caramel. Add the halved apricots and the whole raspberries and turn them in the caramel. Moisten with orange liqueur and flambé. As soon as the alcohol has evaporated, pour the sauce into the center of the coronets and around the edge, and decorate with a dollop of whipped cream. Serve immediately, before the choux puffs become soggy.

Chocolate Bavarois (far left),
Cholocate-glazed Cookies (above)
and Coronets of Choux Puffs (left)

Coconut and Chocolate Bavarois

Bavarese di Cocco e Cioccolato

To serve 8-10

1 coconut

3 cups whipping cream

2¼ cups sugar

2¼ cups milk

1½ tablespoons unflavored gelatin

kirsch

3 egg yolks

1 teaspoon cornstarch

1½ ounces semisweet chocolate

16 strands of fresh coconut

10 strands of candied citrus peel

12 chocolate wafer cigarettes

Preparation time: about 1 hour, plus 8 hours setting and 12 hours infusing

1) Break open the coconut, discard the water, then peel with a vegetable peeler to obtain about 10 ounces flesh. Purée this in food processor.

2) Place the puréed coconut in a saucepan with 1¼ cups of the cream, ¾ cup of the sugar and 1 cup of the milk, then leave to infuse for 12 hours. Soak just over half the gelatin in a bowl of cold water.

3) Place the saucepan containing the coconut mixture over medium heat and heat without boiling, then add the gelatin to the coconut mixture and stir to dissolve. Take the pan off the heat and leave to cool.

4) Press the coconut mixture through a fine strainer lined with cheesecloth. Pour the resulting mixture into a 1½-quart mold brushed with kirsch, then refrigerate.

5) Beat the egg yolks with 6 tablespoons of the sugar and the cornstarch, then gradually pour in the remaining milk, which should be heated. Pour the mixture into a saucepan, add the chocolate and the remaining gelatin.

6) When the mixture begins to thicken, whip the remaining cream and stir it in. Pour this mixture over the set coconut bavarois in the mold. Refrigerate for at least 8 hours before serving.

1

2

3

4

5

6

CAKES

The Italians are masters when it comes to making fabulous cakes — both scrumptious to eat and ravishingly beautiful to look at. Cakes lend style and elegance to any table, so much so that it sometimes seems a shame to destroy such wonderful creations by eating them. Force yourself, though. Don't hold back — it willl be worth every moment for that wonderful explosion of flavors!

Zabaione Charlotte

Charlotte allo Zabaione

To serve 8

6 egg yolks

¹/₂ cup sugar

1 cup Marsala wine

¹/₄ cup sweet white wine

1³/₄ cups whipping cream

4 small cups of strong coffee

42 ladyfingers

cocoa powder

Preparation time: about 40 minutes, plus chilling

Put the egg yolks in a saucepan and add the sugar, Marsala wine and sweet white wine. Place over very low heat and beat continuously until the mixture thickens into a very creamy, foamy zabaione, taking care not to let it boil. Take the pan off the heat, transfer the zabaione to a bowl and leave to cool.

Meanwhile, whip the cream until stiff. When the zabaione is cool, delicately fold in half the whipped cream. Dilute the coffee with a glass of water. Spread out 30 ladyfingers in a dish and pour the coffee over. Line the base of a 7¹/₂-inch, 5-inch deep charlotte mold with waxed paper. Add a layer of coffee-soaked lady fingers. Cover with about one-third of the zabaione. Make a second layer of ladyfingers and continue to make layers in this way, finishing with ladyfingers. Place the mold in the freezer for at least 1 hour.

Unmold the charlotte onto a serving plate, remove the paper and sprinkle the dessert with sifted cocoa powder. Spread a little of the remaining whipped cream over the sides and stick on the 12 unsoaked ladyfingers, spacing them apart. Put the remaining cream into a pastry bag with a fluted tip and decorate the charlotte with a grid of whipped cream on top, and stripes between the ladyfingers. Serve immediately, or keep the charlotte refrigerated until ready to serve.

Zabaione Charlotte (top) and **Pink Pillow** (bottom)

Pink Pillow

Mattonella Rosa

To serve 8

4 eggs, plus 4 extra yolks

³/₄ cup sugar

a pinch of salt

1 teaspoon vanilla extract

1¹/₄ cups all-purpose flour

butter and flour for the pan and waxed paper

1¹/₄ cups milk

maraschino liqueur

12 ounces store-bought frosting

²/₃ cup whipping cream, whipped

Preparation and cooking time: about 12 hours

To make the cake, preheat the oven to 400°F. Beat the 4 whole eggs with half the sugar and ¹/₂ teaspoon of the vanilla, using an electric mixer, until pale and of a ribbon consistency. Sift the salt mixed with the flour lightly over the mixture, then fold it in delicately. Grease a 16- x 13¹/₂-inch jelly-roll pan and line it with waxed paper. Lightly grease and flour the paper, then spread out the cake batter. Bake in the preheated oven for about 15 minutes. Remove the baked jelly roll from the oven, invert it onto a clean cloth towel and leave to cool.

Meanwhile, prepare the pastry cream. Heat the milk and flavor it with the remaining vanilla. Beat the egg yolks with the remaining sugar and remaining ¹/₂ cup flour in a small saucepan, then gradually pour in the hot milk. Place over low heat and cook for about 10 minutes until thickened, stirring continuously with a wooden spoon.

Cut the cooled cake into 3 equal rectangles. Brush one with a little liqueur, then cover with about half the pastry cream. Top with the second cake rectangle and repeat the procedure, reserving a few spoonfuls of pastry cream to decorate the finished dessert. Finish with the third cake rectangle and brush this with liqueur. Spread the reserved pastry cream over the sides of the dessert.

In a bain-marie, melt the fondant frosting to the consistency of thick cream (if necessary, dilute it with a few drops of water) and color it with a dash of liqueur. Pour over the top of the dessert and spread evenly with a spatula. Place the whipped cream in a pastry bag with a fluted tip and decorate the sides of the dessert by piping on lines of whipped cream.

Luscious Cherry Cake

Dolce Cremoso alle Ciliegie

To serve 8

¹/₂ pound fresh cherries

1¹/₄ cup sugar

1 stick cinnamon

1 clove

6 tablespoons dry white wine

1¹/₂ tablespoons unflavored gelatin

2 eggs, plus 2 extra yolks

grated peel of ¹/₂ lemon

a pinch of salt

¹/₂ cup all-purpose flour

2¹/₂ cups milk

1 round cake layer, weighing about 8 ounces

6 tablespoons orange liqueur

Preparation and cooking time: about 1 hour, plus chilling

Stem the cherries, rinse them and drain them well. Remove the pits and place the cherries in a small saucepan. Add ¹/₄ cup of the sugar, a small piece of cinnamon, the clove and the white wine. Cook the cherries over medium heat for about 15 minutes, until they are tender and the liquid has a syrupy consistency; leave to cool.

Meanwhile, dissolve the gelatin in cold water. In a small saucepan, beat the eggs and egg yolks together with the remaining sugar, the lemon peel, salt and the sifted flour. When creamy and smooth, dilute the mixture with the cold milk, poured in a trickle. Place over the heat and, stirring constantly, bring the mixture almost to a boil. Remove from the heat and add the gelatin, stirring to make sure it dissolves.

Line a 10- x 5-inch cake pan with aluminum foil. Pour some of the hot custard sauce into it, then arrange some thin slices of cake on top. Sprinkle lightly with orange liqueur. Spread over a few cooked and drained cherries (the syrup will be used at the end to moisten the cake) over the cake, then cover with some more of the custard sauce, cake and cherries. Continue with the layers until you have used up all the ingredients.

Leave the cake to cool, then place in the refrigerator for at least 2 hours, or in the freezer for about 30 minutes or until the cake is quite firm. Then turn out onto a serving plate, pour the cherry syrup over it and serve.

Strawberry and Orange Cake

Cuore di Mamma

To serve 8-10

2 eggs, plus 3 extra yolks

¾ cup sugar

a little vanilla sugar

a pinch of salt

¾ cup all-purpose flour

½ cup potato flour

a little butter for greasing cake pan

1 tablespoon unflavored gelatin

6 tablespoons dry Marsala wine

1 tablespoon brandy

1 cup whipping cream

1 cup fresh strawberries

6 tablespoons orange liqueur

Preparation and cooking time: about 2 hours, plus at least 2 hours chilling

Preheat the oven to 350°F. Beat 2 whole eggs with ½ cup of the sugar, a little vanilla sugar and the salt until light and fluffy. Sift and fold in all but 2 tablespoons of the flour and the potato flour.

Butter a 7½-cup heart-shaped cake tin, sprinkle in the remaining flour and pour in the batter. Bake for about 20 minutes or until a wooden skewer pushed into the center of the cake comes out clean. Turn out onto a wire rack and leave to cool. Wash the cake pan.

Soak the gelatin in cold water. Beat the 3 egg yolks with the remaining sugar until white and fluffy. Blend in the Marsala wine and then the brandy.

Strawberry and Orange Cake

Heat the mixture and bring it almost to a boil, stirring constantly. Pour the mixture into a bowl and stir in the gelatin immediately. Leave to cool, stirring from time to time. Finally, whip the cream and fold it into the mixture.

Hull and wash the strawberries and slice them finely. Line the bottom of the washed cake pan with waxed paper and brush it with a little orange liqueur. Return the heart-shaped cake to the pan and make holes in it with a fork. Sprinkle with the remaining orange liqueur.

Pour half the prepared gelatin mixture onto the cake and sprinkle it with half the strawberries. Cover with the rest of the mixture and sprinkle with the remaining strawberries. Tap the cake pan gently and place it in the refrigerator for a least 2 hours.

Once the filling has set, run a knife around the edge of the cake and invert it onto a plate. Keep in the refrigerator until ready to serve.

Chocolate-Cream Gateau

Pagoda di Castagne

To serve 8

1¹/₃ cups chestnut purée

---

¹/₂ cup mascarpone cheese or cream cheese

---

1 cup powdered sugar

---

¹/₄ cup cocoa powder

---

2 tablespoons brandy

---

3 tablespoons Amaretto liqueur

---

²/₃ cup whipping cream

---

1 sponge cake, about 9 inches wide

---

¹/₂ cup orange liqueur

---

1 tablespoon chocolate sprinkles

---

1 tablespoon white chocolate chips

---

6 chocolate buttons

Preparation time: about 1¹/₂ hours

Place the chestnut purée in a bowl and beat in the mascarpone cheese, stirring with a wooden spoon until smooth. Sift ³/₄ cup of the powdered sugar and the cocoa powder over, and mix well, then add the brandy and Amaretto liqueur, making sure that each tablespoon is thoroughly absorbed before adding the next.

Whip the cream until stiff, then fold in the rest of the sifted powdered sugar, stirring with a wooden spoon from top to bottom. Spoon the cream into a pastry bag with a small round tip, and keep in the refrigerator.

Place the cake on a serving dish and moisten it with the orange liqueur, then push through a strainer the mixture of chestnuts and mascarpone cheese onto it, arranging it in a small heap. Pipe the sweetened whipped cream around the edge, and sprinkle the chocolate sprinkles over. Complete the decoration of the cake by placing the white chocolate chips on top of it and arranging the chocolate buttons evenly spread around it.

Keep the cake in the refrigerator until serving time. If you wish, instead of using sponge cake as a base, you can use any other kind of risen cake such as panettone, Viennese pastry or so on.

Coffee Cream Puff

Sfogliata alla Crema di Caffè

To serve 10

---

1 pound puff pastry dough

---

¹/₂ cup butter

---

8 almonds

---

1 egg

---

¹/₂ cup mascarpone cheese

---

1 cup powdered sugar

---

2 tablespoons freeze-dried instant coffee

---

2 tablespoons coffee liqueur

---

2 tablespoons brandy

---

12 ladyfingers or plain cookies

---

²/₃ cup Amaretto liqueur

Preparation and cooking time: about 1 hour, plus any thawing

Thaw the dough if necessary. Preheat the oven to 375°F. Cut the butter into small pieces and leave to soften.

Meanwhile, finely chop the almonds. Divide the dough in half and roll it out into two 10-inch circles. Place on 2 baking sheets and prick with a fork all over. Separate the egg yolk from the white and brush the surface of the dough with the white. Bake for about 20 minutes, or until the pastry is golden brown. Remove from the oven and place on a wire rack to cool.

Meanwhile, beat the butter with the mascarpone cheese and the powdered sugar, ideally with an electric mixer. Incorporate the egg yolk, the instant coffee, the coffee liqueur and the brandy. The cream should be light and fluffy by the time you have finished.

Lay one pastry circle on top of the other and trim until they are exactly the same size. (Keep the offcuts.) Place one circle on a round cardboard cake base and spread one-third of the coffee cream over it. Soak the ladyfingers in the Amaretto and arrange these on top of the cream, breaking them up to that they do not jut out. Spread half the remaining cream over the ladyfingers, then sprinkle the crumbled pastry offcuts over and press down the second pastry circle to ensure it adheres to the cream.

Cover the cake with the remaining cream and decorate with the chopped almonds. Place on a cake stand and refrigerate for at least 30 minutes before serving. Finally, sprinkle with a little powdered sugar or decorate as you please.

Orange Tart with Whipped Cream

Crostata all'Arancia con Panna Montata

To serve 6-8

¹/₂ **cup butter**

3 cups all-purpose flour

1 egg, plus 4 extra yolks

1 cup powdered sugar

1 teaspoon ground cinnamon

³/₄ **cup sugar**

5 oranges

2¹/₄ **cups milk**

2 tablespoons orange liqueur

flour and butter for the work surface and pan

1 cup whipping cream

¹/₃ **cup apricot jam**

Preparation and cooking time: about 1¹/₂ hours

First, make the crust. Mix together the butter with 2¹/₂ cups of the flour, then place on the work surface and make a well in the center. Break the egg into the center and add the powdered sugar and the cinnamon. Knead fairly

quickly to prevent the butter softening too much, then wrap the dough in plastic wrap and refrigerate for about 30 minutes.

Meanwhile, make the filling. In a bowl, beat the 4 egg yolks with the sugar, remaining flour and the grated peel of 1 orange. Heat the milk and gradually pour it onto the egg mixture, then pour it back into the pan and place over low heat. Simmer the custard for 5 minutes, stirring continuously to avoid lumps, then add the liqueur and leave to cool.

Preheat the oven to 375°F. On a lightly floured surface, roll out the dough into a ³/₈-inch thick circle. Use it to line a greased and floured 10¹/₂-inch springform cake pan. Fill with the cold custard. Trim off the excess dough from the edges and crimp the border. Bake in the hot oven for about 40 minutes.

Meanwhile, prepare the decoration. Peel 3 oranges, paring off all the white membrane, and cut into slices. Whip the cream very stiffly. Dilute the jam with one-third of a glass of water and boil for 3 minutes. Pare off the peel from the remaining orange and cut into very thin slivers. Blanch in boiling water for 2 minutes and drain thoroughly.

Remove the tart from the oven, unmold it onto a serving plate and leave to cool. Arrange the sliced oranges on the filling and glaze with the warm apricot jam. Fill a pastry bag with a fluted tip with the whipped cream and pipe a border of cream rosettes around the tart. Finish with a sprinkling of orange peel.

Semifreddo Ice Cream Cake with Raspberry Sauce

Semifreddo con Salsa ai Lamponi

To serve 8

5 eggs, 3 separated, plus 1 extra white

2¹/₂ **cups sugar**

a pinch of salt

³/₄ **teaspoon vanilla extract**

1¹/₄ **cups all-purpose flour**

butter and flour for the pan

2¹/₄ **cups milk**

grated peel of 1 lemon

2¹/₂ **cups whipping cream**

maraschino liqueur

4 ounces fresh raspberries

colored sugar shapes

Preparation time and cooking time: about 2 hours, plus freezing

To make the cake layers, preheat the oven to 350°F. Beat 2 eggs and 6 tablespoons of the sugar together with the salt and ¹/₄ teaspoon vanilla until any mixture that falls off the beaters remains on the surface and does not immediately sink back into the batter in the bowl. Sift in ³/₄ cup of the flour from a height, folding it in delicately, working from bottom to top and vice versa. Grease a 16- x 13¹/₂-inch jelly-roll pan, sprinkle with a pinch of flour, then spoon in the cake batter and bake in the preheated oven for 5 minutes. When baked, invert the cake onto a scrupulously clean cloth towel and leave to cool.

Heat the milk without letting it boil, and flavor with the lemon peel and remaining vanilla. In a bowl, beat 4 egg yolks with ³/₄ cup of the sugar and ¹/₂ cup of the flour. Gradually pour in the milk, stirring to prevent lumps from forming, then return the mixture to the pan and place over medium heat. Simmer for 4 to 5 minutes, then take off the heat and leave to cool.

Meanwhile, put 3 egg whites in a bowl with the remaining sugar, then stand the bowl in a saucepan filled with 2 fingers of warm water. Place over medium heat and beat the egg whites until very firm. Whip 1³/₄ cups of the cream separately until very stiff. Delicately fold the whipped cream, maraschino liqueur and the beaten egg whites into the cold custard.

Line the loose bottom of a 9-inch springform cake pan with a circle of waxed paper. Cover the sides with a strip of cake. Pour all the custard into the prepared mold, then cover it with the remaining trimmings from the cake. Cover the pan with thick aluminum foil, then invert the pan and place in the freezer for at least 4 hours.

Just before serving, make a raspberry sauce. Purée the raspberries with the remaining sugar and 1 tablespoon of maraschino liqueur, then transfer to a bowl. Remove the bottom and foil from the mold and unmold the dessert onto a serving plate. Remove the paper circle and decorate the dessert with swirls of whipped cream and sugar shapes. Serve immmediately, accompanied by the raspberry sauce.

Orange Tart with Whipped Cream (opposite) and Semifreddo Ice Cream Cake with Raspberry Sauce (right)

Homemade Golden Raisin Cake

Dolce Casereccio all'Uvetta

To make 2 cakes

about 10 tablespoons butter, plus extra for greasing the mold and pan

3 cups all-purpose flour, plus extra for the mold and pan and mixing with the golden raisins

1 cup golden raisins

3 tablespoons Strega liqueur

3 eggs, separated

³/₄ cup sugar

salt

grated peel of 1 lemon

¹/₄ cup pine nuts

1 teaspoon baking powder

a little powdered sugar

Preparation and cooking time: about 1¹/₄ hours

The above ingredients will make 2 cakes, each to serve 5 to 6 people. Preheat the oven to 350°F. Butter and flour a round, fluted 3-cup mold and a rectangular 9- x 5- inch cake pan. Soak the golden raisins in the Strega liqueur. Melt ¹/₂ cup of the butter and set aside to cool. Beat the egg yolks with the sugar, a pinch of salt and the lemon peel.

When you have a light frothy mixture, incorporate the cooled melted butter, mixing constantly and vigorously. Continue beating for a few minutes, then drain the golden raisins and add these, floured and mixed with the pine nuts. Sift in 2 cups of the flour mixed with the baking powder. Add the vanilla and 2 tablespoons of the Strega in which the golden raisins were soaked.

Beat the egg whites with a pinch of salt until they are stiff, then carefully fold into the batter which should be fairly stiff. Pour half into the mold and pan, shaking them to eliminate air bubbles. Bake the rectangular cake for 30 minutes and the round one for 40 minutes. Remove from the oven and leave to cool.

Before serving, sprinkle one or both cakes with powdered sugar. Serve with cream, or with zabaglione or custard sauce. The cakes can be kept for 3 or 4 days in their mold or pan, covered with foil. Leave in a cool place.

St. Valentine's Heart

Cuore di San Valentino

To serve 6-8

¹/₂ **pound store-bought puff pastry dough**

8 Amaretti cookies

1 cup chestnuts purée

¹/₂ **cup powdered sugar**

2 tablespoons Amaretto liqueur

3 tablespoons mascarpone cheese or cream cheese

1 tablespoon cocoa powder

¹/₃ **cup pine nuts**

¹/₃ **cup golden raisins**

2 eggs

1 cup whipping cream

10 pink sugared almonds

1 tablespoon colored sugar crystals

a little flour

Preparation and cooking time: 1¹/₂ hours, plus any thawing.

Thaw the puff pastry, if necessary, then roll it out to about ¹/₈ inch thick. Roll it around the rolling pin, then unroll it onto a baking sheet. Place a mold or a piece of cardboard cut into a heart shape that almost covers the dough on top, and cut around it with a sharp knife. Discard the dough trimmings. Prick the heart with a fork and chill.

Meanwhile, preheat the oven to 375°F. Crumble 6 of the Amaretti cookies finely and put them in a bowl with the puréed chestnuts, half the sifted powdered sugar, the Amaretto liqueur, the mascarpone cheese and the cocoa powder. Stir until smooth and creamy, then mix in the pine nuts and half the golden raisins. Bind the mixture with the eggs, beating vigorously.

Spread over the puff pastry to about ¹/₂ inch from the edge. Bake on a low shelf for about 20 minutes.

Place the heart on a rack to cool. Meanwhile, crumble the rest of the cookies very finely. Whip the cream until it is quite stiff, then put it into a pastry bag fitted with a round, fluted tip. Pipe rosettes around the edge of the heart. Sift the remaining powdered sugar over the top, then decorate the cake with the rest of the golden raisins, the remaining crumbled cookies, the pink sugared almonds and the colored sugar crystals. Serve immediately.

Love Hearts

Biscottini d'Amore

To serve 6

2 cups all-purpose flour, plus a little extra for rolling

a pinch of salt

a pinch of ground cinnamon

a pinch of ground cloves

grated peel of ¹/₂ **lemon**

6 tablespoons sugar

1 teaspoon baking powder

1 egg

1 teaspoon vanilla extract

¹/₂ **cup, softened and diced, plus a little extra**

1 heaped teaspoon cocoa powder

1 teaspoon brandy

powdered sugar for decorating (optional)

Preparation and cooking time: about 1 hour

Mix the flour with the salt, cinnamon and cloves, lemon peel and sugar. Add the baking powder, then make a well in the center and add the whole egg, the vanilla extract and the butter.

Knead all together quickly to make a smooth, even dough, then divide into 2 pieces, one twice as large as the other. Work 1 heaped teaspoon of sifted cocoa powder into the smaller piece of dough together with the brandy, kneading for a few minutes. Roll the larger piece out on the board sprinkled lightly with flour to a thickness of about ¹/₈ inch. Then cut into shapes using a heart-shaped cookie cutter and arrange them on 1 or 2 buttered and floured baking sheets. Knead together the remaining dough, roll it out and cut out more shapes. Continue until all the dough has been used. Preheat the oven to 350°F.

Now roll out the cocoa-flavored dough and cut smaller heart shapes out of that, placing them centrally on top of the first hearts and pressing them down lightly to keep in place. Bake the cookies in the oven for about 12 minutes or until they are a light golden brown. Remove carefully from the baking sheet using a spatula and allow to cool on a rack. Sprinkle with a little powdered sugar before serving.

Meringue Gateau

Torta Meringata

To serve 10

a little oil for greasing paper

4 eggs, plus 3 extra whites

salt

2 cups powdered sugar, plus extra for sprinking

2 tablespoons butter, diced

vanilla sugar

1 cup all-purpose flour, plus extra for dusting the baking sheet

¹/₂ cup sugar

2¹/₂ cups milk

1 tablespoon cocoa powder

1 tablespoon orange liqueur

1 tablespoon maraschino liqueur

¹/₂ cup whipping cream

Preparation and cooking time: about 4 hours

To prepare the meringue, lightly grease an 11-inch circle of waxed paper with a little oil and place it on a small baking sheet. Preheat the oven to 225°F.

Beat 3 egg whites with a pinch of salt and sift in 1³/₄ cups of the powdered sugar and a little vanilla sugar, a little at a time, beating briskly until the mixture is well risen and firm. Using a pastry bag with a round tip, cover the circle of waxed paper by piping two overlapping spirals. Sprinkle the remaining powdered sugar on top, then bake for a couple of hours; turn off the oven and leave for an hour before taking it out to cool.

To prepare the éclairs, preheat the oven to 375°F, and butter and flour a small baking sheet. Bring 5 tablespoons of water to a boil in a saucepan with the diced butter and a pinch of salt. As soon as the butter is melted, remove from the heat and sift in half the flour, beating briskly with a wooden spoon. Return the pan to the heat and continue to cook, stirring continuously, until the mixture begins to sizzle and comes away from the side of the pan. Turn it out onto a plate and spread it out to cool.

Return the cooled mixture to the pan and beat in 1 egg, making sure the mixture is completely smooth. Using a pastry bag with a round tip, pipe at least 30 finger shapes on the prepared

baking sheet, spaced apart to allow them to spread. Bake for 15 minutes, then turn them out onto a wire rack to cool.

To prepare the custard sauce, beat the remaining eggs, the sugar, a little vanilla sugar, the remaining flour and a pinch of salt together in a saucepan. When smooth, gradually stir in the milk. Bring to a boil, stirring all the time. Remove from the heat and divide into 2 portions, adding the cocoa powder and the orange liqueur to one half, and the maraschino liqueur to the other. Let them cool, stirring frequently, then put them into 2 separate pastry bags with round tips.

To assemble the gateau, whip the cream and pipe it into the éclairs, then sprinkle them with a little powdered sugar. Just before serving, set the meringue base on a large plate, make a ring around the edge with the yellow custard and set the éclairs on it. Cover the rest of the meringue with alternate stripes of both custards and serve.

St. Valentine's Heart (opposite) and
Meringue Gateau (below)

Pistachio and Coffee Cake

Cake con Pistacchio e Caffè

coffee liqueur

4 teaspoons instant coffee granules

¹/₂ cup butter, softened

2¹/₄ cups powdered sugar

4 eggs, separated

a pinch of salt

3¹/₂ cups all-purpose flour

²/₃ cup shelled and finely chopped pistachios

flour and butter for the pan

Preparation and cooking time:
about 1¹/₂ hours

Preheat the oven to 350°F. Heat the liqueur and dissolve the coffee powder in it. Leave to cool. Using an electric mixer, beat the butter with the sugar to a smooth cream. Then add the egg yolks, one at a time. Sift in 2¹/₄ cups of the flour from a height. Beat the egg whites with the salt until they are very stiff.

Divide the cake batter into 2 equal portions; fold half the egg whites and the chopped pistachios into one portion and the cold coffee liqueur and the remaining egg whites into the other. Generously grease and flour a rectangular 12- x 5-inch cake pan and divide it along its length with a piece of cardboard. Put half the pistachio mixture in one section and half the coffee mixture in the other, then reverse the 2 colors. Remove the cardboard divider and bake for 70 minutes.

Fig and Apricot Ring

Torta 'Coroncina'

To serve 8-10

extra butter and flour for the pan

3 eggs

³/₄ cup sugar

4 tablespoons vanilla sugar

a pinch of salt

1 cup all-purpose flour

¹/₂ cup potato flour

3 large, very ripe figs

1¹/₄ cups whipping cream

²/₃ cup orange liqueur

powdered sugar

¹/₃ cup apricot jam

3 sprigs red currants

Preparation and cooking time:
about 1¹/₄ hours

Preheat the oven to 350°F. Butter and flour a round 12-inch cake pan, such as a Kugelhopf pan. Beat the eggs with the sugar, the vanilla sugar and salt until light and fluffy. Stir the flour and the potato flour together, then sift into the mixture. Fold in carefully, using a

Pistachio and Coffee Cake (below)
and Rich Zucotto (opposite)

wooden spoon with an up-and-down motion. Pour into the cake pan and bake for about 30 minutes until a wooden skewer inserted into the cake comes out clean. Turn out onto a wire rack and leave to cool.

Wipe the figs with a damp cloth, then cut them in half and then into very thin slices using a small, very sharp knife. Whip the cream until it is stiff.

Cut the cake into 4 equal layers. Place the bottom layer on a serving dish and pour one-third of the liqueur over. Then spread one-third of the whipped cream over. Sprinkle with 1 teaspoon of powdered sugar. Repeat the procedure with the remaining 2 layers and lightly press on the fourth.

Decorate the top with the fig slices to form a coronet. Melt the apricot jam over low heat and when it is runny, strain through a fine strainer and brush the figs with it. Leave until the jam has cooled. Complete the decoration with the red currants and serve at once.

Rich Zucotto

Zuccotto Ricco

To serve 12

7 egg yolks

1¹⁄₂ cups sugar

salt

1³⁄₄ cups all-purpose flour

¹⁄₂ teaspoon vanilla extract

extra flour and butter for the pan

2¹⁄₄ cups milk

grated peel of ¹⁄₂ lemon

7 ounces semisweet chocolate

1³⁄₄ cups heavy cream

¹⁄₂ cup crème de cacao liqueur

***langue de chat* cookies, for serving**

Preparation and cooking time: about 2 hours, plus 3 hours chilling

Preheat the oven to 375°F. First make a sponge cake. (You can do this the day before.) Beat 3 egg yolks with ³⁄₄ cup of the sugar and a pinch of salt until the batter forms a ribbon. (When you lift the beater, the batter that falls from it does not sink back immediately into the batter in the bowl, but remains lightly on the surface.) Stir in the vanilla, then sift on 1¹⁄₄ cups of the flour from a height, folding it in carefully. Pour the batter into a buttered and floured 9-inch cake pan, then bake in the oven for about 35 minutes, or until a skewer inserted into the center comes out clean. Remove from the oven, invert onto a wire rack and leave to cool.

Meanwhile, make the pastry cream. Beat 4 egg yolks with the remaining sugar and flour. Heat the milk with the lemon peel, then pour it into the egg mixture in a thin stream. Set over medium heat and, stirring continuously, cook for about 5 minutes, then turn off the heat and leave to cool.

Melt 5 ounces of the chocolate and cool until it is warm. Whip one-quarter of the cream until very firm and mix it with the chocolate and the cooled pastry cream.

To assemble the zuccotto, cut the crusts off the cake and slice it. Moisten with the liqueur diluted with ¹⁄₂ cup water. Use some of the slices to line a large, flat-bottomed bowl. Cut the rest into strips and fill the bowl with layers of chocolate cream and sponge strips. Chill in the refrigerator for at least 3 hours.

Unmold the zuccotto onto a serving plate. Whip the remaining cream, place in a pastry bag with a ridged tip, and pipe it over the zuccotto. Melt the rest of the chocolate, place in a parchment cone and decorate the zuccotto, finishing with a crown of *langues de chat* cookies. Leave in the refrigerator until ready to serve; the decorated zuccotto will keep for 6 to 8 hours.

Mother's Day Cake

Torta "Festa della Mamma"

To serve 10-12

butter and extra flour for the pan

1 cup all-purpose flour

3 eggs, plus 4 extra yolks

1¹/₂ cups sugar

4 tablespoons vanilla sugar

a pinch of salt

¹/₂ cup potato flour

1 tablespoon unflavored gelatin

²/₃ cup Marsala wine

¹/₂ cup Amaretto liqueur

¹/₂ cup whipping cream

5 large, ripe strawberries

Preparation and cooking time:
about 1¹/₄ hours, plus at least 2 hours chilling

Preheat the oven to 350°F. Butter and flour a springform cake pan about 10-inches in diameter. Beat 3 eggs with ³/₄ cup of the sugar, half the vanilla sugar and the salt until frothy. Add the flour and the potato flour sifted together. Fold them in very gently with an up-and-down movement, rather than a circular one. Pour the batter into the cake pan and bake in the oven for about 35 minutes, or until a skewer inserted into the center comes out clean. Turn the cake out onto a rack to cool.

Meanwhile, soften the gelatin in a little cold water. In a copper bowl, beat the 4 egg yolks together with the remaining sugar and vanilla sugar. When the mixture is frothy, add the Marsala wine, making sure that each tablespoon is thoroughly absorbed before adding the next. Then add 3 tablespoons of the Amaretto liqueur, pouring it in a trickle and stirring all the time. Place the copper bowl over a pan of barely simmering water and, still stirring, heat the zabaglione cream until it is very hot. At this point remove it from the heat and fold in the gelatin. Mix thoroughly until the gelatin dissolves, then pour the zabaglione cream into a bowl and let it cool.

Cut the cake into 3 layers of equal thickness and place the lowest one back in the pan used to bake it in, lined with waxed paper. Sprinkle the cake with one-third of the remaining Amaretto liqueur and spread one-third of the warm zabaglione cream over. Repeat the procedure with the second and third layers of cake. Refrigerate the cake for a least 2 hours, when the zabaglione cream will have set.

Beat the cream until stiff and put it in a pastry bag. Wipe the strawberries and hull 4 of them, then cut them in half lengthwise. Slide the blade of a small knife between the side of the pan and the cake, then open the hinge and detach the side of the pan. Slide the cake onto a serving dish by removing first the bottom of the pan and then the waxed paper. Decorate the top with the whipped cream and the strawberries. Serve immediately.

Festive Dove

Colomba Augurale

To serve 8

a little butter and flour for the pan

3 eggs, plus 6 extra yolks

1³/₄ cups sugar

¹/₄ teaspoon honey

2 tablespoons vanilla sugar

a pinch of salt

1 cup all-purpose flour

¹/₂ cup potato flour

2¹/₂ cups milk

1 tea bag

Preparation and cooking time:
about 1¹/₂ hours

Preheat the oven to 350°F. Butter and flour a dove-shaped cake pan, about 7¹/₂-cups in capacity. Beat the 3 whole eggs with ³/₄ cup of the sugar, the honey, the vanilla sugar and salt, until smooth and frothy. Stir the flour and potato flour together, then sift them into the sugar and egg mixture. Fold in with a wooden spoon using an up-and-down movement, rather than a circular one. Pour evenly into the pan and bake for about 30 minutes, until a skewer comes out clean. Remove the pan from the oven and, after a few minutes, turn the dove out onto a wire rack.

While the cake is cooling, make the custard sauce. Set aside 4 tablespoons of the milk and pour the rest into a saucepan. Bring gradually to a boil and remove from the heat. Put in the tea bag and leave to infuse for 5 minutes. Remove the tea bag, squeezing it thoroughly, then discard it.

Beat the egg yolks with the remaining sugar until you obtain a frothy mixture. Then stir in first the reserved cold milk and then the tea-flavored milk, poured in gradually through a fine strainer. Mix in with a small balloon whisk. Heat the saucepan gently and bring the custard sauce to just below boiling point, taking care not to let it actually boil. Remove from the heat at once and immerse in cold water, stirring continuously until the custard sauce has cooled.

Pour the custard sauce into a

pitcher or bowl and serve with the dove. Decorate the dove as you please.

Chocolate and Nut Gateau

Veneziana con Panna e Castasgne

To serve 10

2¹/₄-pound large, round brioche, panettone or plain cake

12 ounces chestnuts, peeled and boiled

4 ounces semisweet chocolate

¹/₃ cup walnuts

1¹/₄ cups whipping cream

1 cup powdered sugar

²/₃ cup rum

1 candied chestnut

Preparation time: about 1 hour

Cut the cake into 3 equal layers. Purée the chestnuts (or use a can of already puréed unsweetened chestnuts.) Finely chop the chocolate and the walnuts. Whip the cream until stiff, then sift in 6 tablespoons of the powdered sugar, stirring with a top-to-bottom folding movement to avoid deflating the cream.

Place a layer of the cake on a serving plate, moisten it with half the rum, then spread it with half the whipped cream and half the chestnut purée, topped with half the chocolate and walnuts. Cover with the second layer of cake and fill in the same way. Cover with the top layer, place a small bowl in the center and sprinkle the remaining powdered sugar over the exposed surface of the cake. Remove the bowl and carefully place the candied chestnut in the center of the cake.

Serve as soon as possible without refrigerating. If you prefer, the cake may be cut into more layers, in which case the filling ingredients should be divided equally among all the layers.

Festive Dove

Panettone Charlotte

Charlotte di Panettone

To serve 8

about 1 pound apples

about 1¹/₂ pounds pears

¹/₂ cup butter, plus extra for the bowl

¹/₂ cup sugar

²/₃ cup dry white wine

12 ounces panettone which has become a little hard

2 eggs

²/₃ cup milk

¹/₂ cup heavy cream

Preparation and cooking time: about 2¹/₂ hours, plus cooling and chilling

Preheat the oven to 350°F. Peel, core and quarter the apples and pears. Heat 2 skillets with about ¹/₄ cup of the butter in each. As soon as the butter has melted, put the apples in one skillet and the pears in the other. Sprinkle each with 1 tablespoon of sugar and pour half the wine into each skillet. Cook over low heat until the fruit is cooked but still firm and the pieces intact.

Meanwhile, liberally butter a 7¹/₂-cup bowl that is ovenproof, then cut 2 foil strips, about 2 inches wide and long enough to place crosswise inside the bowl with about ³/₄ inch at the ends to hang over the rim. Butter these, too.

Cut the panettone into thin slices. Place a layer of panettone on the bottom of the bowl and press it down lightly to make it stick. Then place half the apples on top. Cover with another layer of panettone and then a layer of pears. Continue alternating the panettone, apples and pears in this way, finishing with a layer of panettone. Press down lightly so there are no spaces left.

Beat the eggs with the remaining sugar in a bowl and dilute with the milk and cream. Pour the mixture over the panettone and prick with a skewer to help the liquid penetrate. Leave the charlotte to rest for about 15 minutes,

then bake it for about 1¹/₂ hours. Remove from the oven and leave to cool.

Turn it out onto a serving dish with the help of the strips of foil, which should then be discarded. Refrigerate the charlotte for a couple of hours before serving. This is a particularly good recipe for using up leftover panettone.

Panettone Filled with Mandarin Orange Custard

Panettone Farcito al Mandarino

To serve 10-12

about 2 tablespoons unflavored gelatin

4 eggs

¹/₂ cup sugar

grated peel of 1 mandarin orange

¹/₂ cup flour

1¹/₄ cups milk

¹/₂ cup mandarin juice

1 panettone

4 tablespoons orange liqueur

1³/₄ cups whipping cream

Preparation and cooking time: about 1 hour, plus 6-8 hours chilling

Dissolve the gelatin in cold water. Beat together the egg yolks and the sugar in a saucepan until pale and frothy. Add the mandarin orange peel, then sift in the flour. Stir again, then dilute with the milk and mandarin juice, adding them in a trickle. Bring slowly to a boil, stirring constantly with a wooden spoon. Remove from the heat and dissolve the gelatin in the mixture. Leave to cool, stirring gently from time to time to prevent a skin from forming.

Meanwhile, turn the panettone upside-down and, using a sharp, pointed knife, cut out a circle from the bottom, about ³/₄ inch from the edge. Make a large cavity and pour in the liqueur. Whip the cream and fold it into the cold mandarin-flavored custard sauce. Use an up-and-down movement, not a circular one, to

prevent the cream from going flat. Pour the mixture into the panettone and replace the circle in the bottom to restore its original form. Place it upside-down in a bowl that is just the right size to hold the panettone, then cover with plastic wrap.

Refrigerate for 6 to 8 hours or, better still, overnight. Turn out onto a serving dish and serve. Cut with a sharp, serrated knife to avoid crumbling the panettone.

Panettone with Sauce

Salsa ai Panettone

To serve 12

10 ounces mixed berries, such as strawberries, raspberries and blueberries

1¹/₂ cups sugar

¹/₄ cup orange liqueur

1 x 2¹/₄-pound panettone

Preparation time: about 10 minutes, plus overnight marinating

Pick over the fruits and discard any that are bruised, then rinse them thoroughly and drain well. Marinate overnight in the sugar and liqueur.

Just before serving, crush the fruits with a small balloon whisk, leaving them in the marinade, and mix to make a thick sauce. Transfer to a bowl and bring to the table for your guests to help themselves. Slice the panettone into plain pieces (as it comes in the box), or cut into ³/₄-inch slices and briefly toast in a very hot oven. Serve accompanied by the fruit sauce.

Panettone Filled with Mandarin Orange Custard (top) and *Panettone Charlotte* (bottom)

Homemade Apple Cake

Torta di Mele, Casereccia

To serve 8

2 eggs

³/₄ cup caster sugar

salt

grated peel of 1 lemon

a pinch of ground cinnamon

a pinch of ground cloves

1¹/₄ cups all-purpose flour

¹/₄ cups cornstarch

5 tablespoons milk

1 teaspoon baking powder

butter for greasing the pan, plus a little extra

bread crumbs

1 pound apples, just ripe

¹/₄ cup apricot jam

Preparation and cooking time:
about 1¹/₂ hours, plus cooling

Preheat the oven to 350°F. Beat the eggs with 1¹/₂ cups of the sugar, a pinch of salt and the lemon peel. Then add another pinch of salt, followed by the cinnamon and the cloves. Combine the flour and the cornstarch and sift these into the mixture. Gradually pour in the milk and sift in the baking powder. Mix all these ingredients together to form a smooth batter.

Butter a 10-inch cake pan and sprinkle it with bread crumbs. Pour in the batter. Peel and halve the apples, core and slice them, not too thinly. Arrange the slices on top of the batter. Sprinkle with the remaining sugar and intersperse with slivers of butter. Bake for about 45 minutes, or until a toothpick comes out clean. Remove the cake from the oven and leave to cool on a wire rack.

Heat the apricot jam over low heat and, when it has melted, brush the surface of the cake with it and leave to cool. This cake is best eaten the same day.

Cherry Jelly Roll

Roulade di Ciliegie

To serve 6

2 eggs

6 tablespoons sugar

¹/₂ teaspoon vanilla essence

³/₄ cup all-purpose flour

butter for greasing the pan and waxed paper

1¹/₄ cups whipping cream

powdered sugar

orange-flower water

9 ounces cherries

Preparation and cooking time:
about 40 minutes, plus chilling

To make the cake, preheat the oven to 400°F. Beat the eggs with the sugar and vanilla until light and fluffy, then sift in the flour from a height and fold it in.

Grease a 16- x 13¹/₂-inch jelly-roll pan, line it with a sheet of waxed paper and lightly grease the paper. Pour in the cake batter, then bake in the preheated oven for about 10 minutes.

Remove the cake from the oven and invert it onto a scrupulously clean cloth towel. Peel off the paper, roll up the cake in the cloth and leave to cool.

Meanwhile, whip the cream very stiffly and flavor with 1 tablespoon of powdered sugar and 1 tablespoon of orange-flower water.

Rinse the cherries, drain well and pit them, using a cherry pitter. Cut them into small pieces.

Unroll the jelly roll and spread the cream over. Sprinkle with the chopped cherries, then roll up again. Wrap the jelly roll in a sheet of waxed paper and refrigerate for at least 4 hours before serving. Cut the jelly roll into even slices and arrange these on a serving plate, decorating as you wish.

INDEX